ISLAMIC SURVEYS 9

THE INFLUENCE OF ISLAM ON MEDIEVAL EUROPE

W. MONTGOMERY WATT

EDINBURGH
at the University Press

EDINBURGH UNIVERSITY PRESS
22 George Square, Edinburgh

ISBN 0 85224 218 2

North America
Aldine · Atherton, Inc.
529 South Wabash Avenue, Chicago

Library of Congress
Catalog Card Number 70-182902

Printed in Great Britain by
T. & A. Constable Ltd, Edinburgh

FOREWORD

This series of Islamic Surveys was launched about ten years ago with the aim of 'giving the educated reader something more than can be found in the usual popular books'. The general idea was that each work should survey some part of the vast field covered by Islamic Studies, not merely presenting an outline of what was known and generally accepted, but also indicating the points at which scholarly debate continued. A bibliography, preferably annotated, was to guide the reader who wished to pursue his study further. The series has advanced more slowly than was hoped, but to judge from the reception of the volumes so far published, the general aim has been realized fairly well. We have not yet managed to include in the series all the volumes we should have liked to include, and we have added some that were not originally thought of.

The present volume falls into this latter category. When I was invited to deliver a series of lectures as visiting professor at the Collège de France in December 1970, a variety of circumstances led me to choose the topic of Islamic influences on Europe. Since lectures of this type are in themselves a survey of a special field, it seemed not inappropriate to print as it stood the English text from which the French was prepared. In accordance with the aim of the series, however, there have been added footnotes which contain an annotated bibliography of the Islamic aspects and some additional material; but no attempt has been made to give a comparable bibliography for the European aspects, though the main works on which I depended here have been mentioned. The French text of the lectures and annotations is being published in the *Revue des Études Islamiques*, the first two lectures being in vol. XXXIX (1971).

I am deeply grateful to M. Henri Laoust and the governing

body of the Collège de France for the invitation which gave me the privilege of lecturing there. I should also like to take this opportunity of thanking M. Laoust and his colleagues, especially M. and Mme Sourdel and Mme Beldiceanu, for all the kindness they showed me while I was in Paris. I am indebted to Professors Geoffrey Barraclough of Cambridge and Gordon Donaldson of Edinburgh for reading and commenting on an earlier essay on a similar subject, though they are of course not responsible for the views I have expressed. Mlle Marie-Thérèse d'Alverny kindly read the text of the fifth lecture and saved me from a number of errors.

In so far as transliteration has been necessary, I have followed the system used in the other volumes of the series, but as far as possible I have employed the europeanized forms of the names.

W. Montgomery Watt

THE CONTENTS

ONE

ISLAMIC PRESENCE IN EUROPE

The aim

The various ways in which the Islamic world influenced medieval Europe have been studied by scholars, and the results of their studies are to be found in many scholarly books and articles. There has been hardly any attempt, however, to look at this Islamic influence in its totality and to assess the importance of its contribution to Europe and of Europe's response to it.[1] The aim of this present series of lectures is therefore to give a comprehensive view of this influence and of the reaction to it. I must emphasize at the outset, however, that this view will be given from the standpoint of an Islamist and not of a historian of medieval Europe. For one thing this means that I shall speak as an amateur without any professional competence in European history, and must therefore crave indulgence for any shortcomings in this aspect of my subject. For another it means that my perspective will be different from that of the European historian. I shall not think of the Muslims as making yet another alien intrusion into Europe. I shall rather think of them as representatives of a civilization with great achievements to its credit over a large part of the earth's surface, whose benefits here overflow into a neighbouring territory. In all this I shall be concerned almost exclusively with Western Europe or Latin Christendom.

A study of the influence of Islam on Europe is especially relevant at the present time when Christians and Muslims, Europeans and Arabs, are becoming increasingly involved with one another in the 'one world'. It has been recognized for some time that Medieval Christian writers created an image of Islam that was in many respects denigratory, but through the efforts of scholars over the last century or so a more objective picture is now taking shape in the minds of occidentals. For our cultural indebtedness to Islam, however, we Europeans have a blind spot. We sometimes belittle the extent and importance of Islamic influence in our heritage, and sometimes overlook it altogether. For the sake of good relations with Arabs and Muslims we must acknowledge our indebtedness to the full. To try to cover it over and deny it is a mark of false pride.

The Muslim invasion of Spain[2]

Islamic cultural influence on Europe mostly followed on the occupation of Spain and Sicily by Muslims. The beginnings of the military impact may be dated to July 710 when a party of Muslims, about four hundred in number, crossed from North Africa to the southernmost tip of Spain. This was no more than a reconnaissance in force, but the reports the party took back were encouraging, and in the following year (711) a serious and successful attempt at invasion was made. The invading army consisted of 7000 men, shortly afterwards reinforced by a further 5000, but it was so effective that in July 711 it decisively defeated the Visigothic king, Roderick, and thereby destroyed the central administration of his kingdom. There was no further resistance to the Muslims except at local level. By about 715 they had occupied all the main towns of Spain or (in a few cases) entered into treaty relationships with the local rulers. Among the places occupied was Narbonne in the south of France, since this town and the surrounding region had formed part of the Visigothic kingdom. Spain was organized as a province of the Arab empire with a governor who was usually responsible not directly to the caliph in Damascus but to the governor of North Africa based at Cairouan in Tunisia. The country settled down under Arab rule and was mostly at peace. Occasionally there was fighting between different factions among the Muslims.

In 750 the control of the Islamic empire passed from the Umayyad dynasty with their capital at Damascus to the ʿAbbāsids who moved the capital eastwards to their new city of Baghdad. Because their power was based on the eastern half of the empire they had difficulty in gaining recognition in the western provinces. Long before their emissaries reached Morocco, a young Umayyad prince who had escaped there when the rest of his family was put to death was invited to Spain by one of two rival factions. With him at its head this faction was successful, and in 756, as the emir ʿAbd-ar-Raḥmān I, he became the first of the Umayyad dynasty of Cordova. Islamic Spain thus ceased to be a province of the empire and became an independent state, but it retained economic and cultural ties with the rest of the Islamic world. The Umayyad princes gradually produced a measure of unity among the diverse elements in the country, and brought most of it under the control of the central government. Narbonne, however, was lost soon after 750 and Barcelona in 801; and Umayyad jurisdiction did not extend to the wilder districts in the north of modern Spain. The effective limits of Muslim power were marked by the three bases of Saragossa, Toledo and Mérida. Frequent summer expeditions went out from these to 'show the flag' in the disputed regions farther north.

Islamic Spain is usually held to have reached the height of its power and prosperity in the reign of ʿAbd-ar-Raḥmān III (912–61). In the first twenty years of his reign he overcame various threats to the unity of the realm; and by the time of his death he had established his authority over most of the Iberian peninsula, even being acknowledged as suzerain by the small Christian states which had now appeared. The prosperity continued under his son and grandson, but the latter allowed power to slip from his hands into those of his chamberlain, usually known as Almanzor (al-Manṣūr). When Almanzor's son died in 1008, no one appeared to be capable of maintaining the unity of Islamic Spain, and the Umayyad state disintegrated. By 1031 there were some thirty independent local rulers, and the period of 'party kings' (*reyes de taifas*) had begun. Despite the political troubles a measure of prosperity remained, and art and letters flourished on account of the rivalries of the various rulers. The dissension among the Muslims favoured the Christian advance, and in 1085 the important stronghold of Toledo fell.

Some influential Muslim leaders, realizing the serious threat from the Christians, now appealed to the Almoravids (al-Murābiṭūn), the rulers of an extensive Berber empire in north-west Africa. The Almoravids defeated a Christian army and ruled Islamic Spain from about 1090 to 1145. They were then succeeded in both Africa and Spain by an even stronger Berber dynasty, the Almohads (al-Muwaḥḥidūn), who may be said to have ruled Islamic Spain until 1223. After that date the Almohads became involved in dynastic quarrels and withdrew from Spain, so that the Christian kingdoms were able to make rapid progress. Outstanding successes were the capture of Cordova in 1236 and Seville in 1248. By the time matters had quietened down some twenty years later, the only Islamic state left in Spain was the small kingdom of Granada, ruled by the Naṣrid dynasty. Granada achieved a high standard in Arabic literature, though it produced no outstanding work; but it was responsible for one of the great architectural monuments of Islamic Spain, the Alhambra. It maintained its independence until 1492 when it was incorporated in the united kingdom of Aragon and Castile.

The Arabs in Sicily and Italy[3]

Latin Christendom also felt the military impact of the Muslims through Sicily. The first raid on Sicily is recorded in 652 when the city of Syracuse was plundered. This was soon after the Arabs acquired a fleet capable of standing up to the Byzantine fleet. Further raids followed, but until the early ninth century the energies of the Muslims were occupied in other directions. In 800 the province of Ifrīqiyya (corresponding to Tunisia) came into the hands of the Aghlabid family, who nominally governed it for the ʿAbbāsid caliph in Baghdad, but in fact were largely independent. In 827 an appeal from one faction in a Sicilian quarrel gave the Aghlabids an opportunity of invading the island. Palermo was captured in 831 and Messina about 843, though Syracuse did not fall until 878 and the occupation of the island was not complete until about 902. Long before this the Arabs in their usual fashion had pushed onwards with their raiding expeditions. Quarrels between rival Lombard leaders on the mainland of Italy gave an excuse for intervention. In 837 the Arabs were at Naples. In 841 or 847 they occupied Bari, north of Brindisi on the Adriatic, and held it as a forward base for thirty years. In 846 and 849 Rome itself was threatened but not captured; and Pope John VIII (872–82) appears to have paid tribute to the Muslims for two years.

During the ninth century Arab raiders seem to have penetrated through the Alpine passes into central Europe, but the details are obscure. A revival of Byzantine power in southern Italy led, before the end of the century, to the ending of all permanent occupation of the mainland by the Arabs. The Arab hold on Sicily, however, grew tighter. When the Aghlabid dynasty was expelled from Tunisia by the Fāṭimids in 909, Sicily became a Fāṭimid province. An Arab governor installed by the Fāṭimids in 948 became largely independent, for the Fāṭimids became interested in moving eastwards, conquered Egypt in 969 and then transferred the seat of their government to Cairo. Under this governor and his successors, the Kalbite dynasty, Sicily was well ruled and prospered greatly, and Islamic culture took firm root.

The occupation of Sicily did not last as long as that of Spain. In the first half of the eleventh century various Norman knights discovered that they could make a good living in southern Italy as mercenaries or as what might be called independent military entrepreneurs. Their military efficiency was such that a few hundred knights under Robert Guiscard defeated the Byzantines and established a Norman principality. In 1060 his brother Roger led an invasion of Sicily which captured Messina, and proceeded to the occupation of the entire island by 1091. Roger was Count of Sicily until his death in 1101. In the reconquest of Sicily material motives seem to have been stronger than religious ones, and in many respects it remained a part of the Islamic world. The externals of the life of some of the later rulers seemed to contemporaries more Muslim than Christian. In particular Roger's son Roger II (1130–54) and the latter's grandson Frederick II of Hohenstaufen (1215–50) have been called 'the two baptized sultans of Sicily'.

The motives of Arab expansion[4]

Although to the inhabitants of Spain the invasion of 711 may have come as a bolt from the blue, to the Muslims it was the normal continuation of a process that had been going on since the lifetime of Muḥammad. This process came about through a transformation of the nomadic razzia. For centuries nomadic Arab tribes had been in the habit of making raids or razzias on other tribes. The usual aim was to drive off the camels or other livestock of the opponents. The favourite plan was to make a surprise attack with overwhelming force on a small section of the other tribe. In such circumstances it was no disgrace to the persons attacked if they made their escape; and so in many razzias there was little loss of life. Occasionally, however, things might take a more serious turn. After Muḥammad went to Medina in 622 some of his followers, especially those who had emigrated with him from Mecca, began to engage in what were really razzias. Perhaps it was to encourage others to join in the razzias that the Qur'ān spoke of this as 'fighting in the way of God' or 'striving in the way of God'. The Arabic word for 'striving' or 'making efforts to secure a particular aim' is *jāhada* with the verbal noun *jihād*. While the latter can be used of moral and spiritual effort, it has come to be specially associated with fighting against the infidel and is then translated 'holy war'.[5] Although this translation is appropriate, I propose to retain the term Jihād here, since there are differences between the Islamic conception of the Jihād and the Christian conception of the Crusade.

In view of the development of the Jihād out of the nomadic razzia, it is likely that many of the participants were moved more by material cupidity than by religious zeal. The chief distinction between the Jihād and the razzia was in the strategic implications. A nomadic tribe never launched a razzia against a group with which it was allied. In various ways the Muslims at Medina functioned as a tribe or federation of tribes. As Muḥammad's power and authority grew and many tribes and smaller groups wanted to be in alliance with him, he demanded that they should become Muslims and acknowledge him as prophet. In this way before his death in 632 he had built up a vast confederation of tribes and parts of tribes embracing much of Arabia. In the early years the Jihād had been directed against neighbouring pagan tribes not in alliance with the Muslims; but in course of time most of these realized that the simplest way to avoid Muslim attacks was themselves to profess Islam and join the confederation. Since members of the confederation could not raid one another, the energies of the nomadic tribes, which had formerly found an outlet in the razzia, had to be given fresh objects to raid, and this meant going ever farther afield. Thus the practice of the Jihād, in so far as the Muslims were victorious, led both to the continuous growth of the Islamic confederation and to a constant territorial expansion.

This last assertion does not mean that the religion of Islam spread by the sword. In Arabia, indeed, pagan idol-worshipping tribes who became the object of the Jihād were given a choice between Islam and the sword. There was a different treatment, however, for Jews, Christians, Zoroastrians and others reckoned to be monotheists. Their religions were held to be sister religions to Islam, though it was alleged that the contemporary adherents of each had departed from its original purity. Nevertheless they were still monotheists, and could be accepted by Muslims as allies of a sort. In the countries outside Arabia first invaded by Arabs most of the inhabitants were taken to be monotheists. The aim of the Jihād then became not the conversion of these populations but their submission to Muslim rule with the status of protected persons; collectively they were *ahl adh-dhimma*, and the individual was a *dhimmī*. The unit was a group professing the same religion, and they had internal autonomy under their religious head, such as patriarch or rabbi. A poll-tax had to be paid to the Muslim governor for each individual in the group, and various other sums in accordance with the terms of the treaty with the group in question. Sometimes they were less severely taxed than under the previous rulers, and it was a matter of honour for the Islamic state to protect them effectively. In general the situation of the protected groups was not unpleasant, but there were some disadvantages. They were not allowed to bear arms or marry Muslim women, and they were usually excluded from the highest offices of the state. Because of these disadvantages a *dhimmī* might feel he was a second-class citizen; and it appears to be this feeling above all which through the centuries has produced a steady trickle of conversions from Christianity to Islam. Muslims have seldom boasted about conversions to Islam; and in the late seventh century some Muslim leaders actually discouraged conversion because it reduced the poll-tax and upset the budget.

Thus militarily the Jihād led to the expansion of the Islamic empire, but it did not directly lead to conversions. The local administration among the protected groups was usually retained, and this practice made possible the rapid and efficient organization of a great empire. The Arabs only concerned themselves with the central government of each province and the collection of taxes from the protected groups. At first all Muslims received an annual stipend from the treasury, and were then able to devote themselves entirely to the Jihād or other public duties. The system broke down towards 750, but was still effective when Spain was invaded.

From the standpoint of the Muslims the crossing of the straits of Gibraltar in 711 was part of the process of expansion that had been going on for three-quarters of a century. It was one more in a series of raiding expeditions which had been pushing ever farther afield. These might be thought of as Jihād or 'striving in the way of God', but the acquiring of booty was a large part of the motive. After experiencing one or more such raiding expeditions the inhabitants of the countries traversed usually surrendered and became protected allies. Since it was too far for the Arabs to return to Arabia or even Damascus after each campaign, they established camp-cities such as Cairouan. These often became centres of administration and populous urban communities. From them further raiding expeditions went out, and in due course more advanced bases were established. This was what happened in Spain, except that existing towns were used as bases. Despite their limited manpower the Arabs were able within two or three years to occupy the chief towns and achieve a measure of pacification. The local population mostly submitted and received the status of protected allies.

Before the occupation of Visigothic Spain was complete some Arab leaders began to take raiding parties into the Rhone valley and south-west France from bases at Narbonne and Pamplona. In 732 a raiding expedition of this kind penetrated to between Poitiers and Tours, and there was defeated by Charles Martel. This has been acclaimed as one of the decisive battles of the world, and in a sense it is, since it marked the utmost extent of Muslim expansion in this direction. On the other hand, from the account just given of how the Muslim advance came about it should be clear that there was no question of the Arabs of Spain receiving the *coup de grâce*. On the contrary Islamic Spain remained strong for centuries and even for a time increased in strength. What the battle showed was that the Muslims had come to the limit of profitable raiding expeditions. The manpower they could spare to send into central France was insufficient to overcome the opposition they were likely to meet there. Had their military strength increased the Arabs might have ventured north again; but some ten years after the battle insurrections began in the Middle East which marked the death-throes of the Umayyad caliphate, and because of this the Arabs of Spain had no energy to spare for raids far afield. Later, when Spain had become a separate state under an Umayyad emir, all his efforts had to be directed to unifying and pacifying the country. Thus Tours marked the farthest point reached by the tide of Arab expansion in this direction, and the beginning of its ebb.

The Byzantine empire was exposed to this same expansionist pressure from the Muslims. When the Arabs first burst out of Arabia, they gained several victories over Byzantine armies and rapidly occupied the rich provinces of Syria and Egypt. For long they sent raiding expeditions almost annually into the Byzantine territories in Asia Minor. Constantinople itself was attacked in 669, and further threatened by land and sea for several years up to 680. Just after the invasion of Spain it was closely besieged for a whole year (716–7). This pressure on the Byzantine empire continued indefinitely, though in some periods it was greater than in others. It did not affect Latin Christendom directly, but the Popes and other western leaders were aware of it and it influenced their policies at certain points. The impact of the Islamic world was felt in western Europe mainly through Spain and to a lesser extent Sicily.

The distinctive character of the Arab impact

There is a temptation for the historian of Europe, after he has given an account of the invasions by Germans and Slavs, Magyars and Norsemen, to think of the Arab conquest of Spain as a comparable 'barbarian' invasion. Though it is now realized that there was much of value for the building of Europe in the political and social traditions of the so-called barbarian invaders, the temptation to equate the Arabs with the others must, if truth is to prevail, be sternly repressed. At the moment of conquest, indeed, the Arabs and their Berber associates were not obviously at a higher cultural level than the other invaders, but there was an essential difference. The other invaders belonged to societies whose organization was still (in a wide sense) on a tribal basis and which had never known the culture and sophistication associated with great urban developments. The Arabs, on the other hand, were representatives of an empire which in the next century or two became the bearer of the highest culture and civilization in the whole vast region from the Atlantic to Afghanistan.

There is something almost incredible and, because of that, fascinating in the story of how the ancient cultures of theMiddle East became transformed into Islamic culture.[6] In 632, when Muḥammad died and the great expansion had not begun, the Arabs were a relatively primitive people who had few material possessions and whose literary wealth was no more than a tradition of poetry and oratory, together with the sacred book, the Qur'ān, which Muslims reverenced as the speech of God himself conveyed to them by Muḥammad. When Arabs invaded Spain eighty years later, their cultural level cannot have risen greatly, and that of the numerous Berbers in the Muslim armies was probably still lower. In their expansion into Iraq, Syria and Egypt, however, the Arabs had added to their dominions several of the great intellectual centres of the Middle East. Many of the bearers of the previous cultures became Muslims, and an intellectual ferment began which was to last for centuries. In this region of the world mankind had had experience of millennia of urban civilization, going back to Sumer and Akkad and Pharaonic Egypt, and all that had been retained as valuable from these millennia now came to be expressed in Arabic.

When the Romans added the Greek lands to their empire, the result was, as a Latin poet put it, that 'captured Greece took her fierce conqueror captive'. There were some translations into Latin, but on the whole Greek remained the language of learning. The Arab conquests, however, did not lead to the Arabs being 'taken captive' in this way. Instead they imposed their language and something of their outlook on most of the peoples of the empire, although many of the latter were at a higher cultural level. To this result the intense pride and self-confidence of the Arabs contributed. True nomadic Arabs believed that as men they were superior to all others; and something of this pride came to be attached to Islam, which Muslims regarded as the highest and purest form of the worship of God. This superiority was not vociferously insisted on out of any feeling of uncertainty, but was quietly and constantly assumed with serene self-confidence. The wisdom of other peoples was sometimes taken over without acknowledgement, and regarded as coming from an Arab source. In an anecdote about Muḥammad, for example, he is said to have commended to his followers a prayer which is virtually the Lord's Prayer (Paternoster) of the Christians.[7] This process of the assimilation of alien wisdom and learning took place at a deep level, and was not just superficial. When men educated in the previous intellectual traditions became Muslims, they had in their own thinking to fuse their former learning with their Qur'ānic studies. Their contributions went into the general stream of Islamic thought, and thus an autonomous Islamic culture took shape.

The assimilation of alien learning was only possible because at the same time a central core for the new culture was developing naturally out of the main interests of the Arab Muslims.[8] In the second half of the seventh century when there was already an empire of moderate size, religious-minded Arabs would discuss the application to contemporary problems of Qur'ānic rules and the precise relevance to these problems of Muḥammad's example. Out of such discussions, which often took place in the mosque, there developed the great corpus of Islamic law and the science of jurisprudence. Anecdotes about Muḥammad's sayings and doings – technically known as 'Traditions' (*ḥadīth*) – were regarded as normative and were carefully preserved and handed on. Indeed the study of Traditions became one of the major disciplines in Islamic higher education, with various subordinate disciplines attached to it, such as the study of the biographies of the scholars responsible for handing on the anecdotes, and the study of the career of Muḥammad. Not far removed from these was the study of the history and geography of the Islamic lands.

Coupled with the study of the Traditions was the study of the Qur'ān. It is probably true to say that the Qur'ān has a more fundamental place in Islam than the Bible has in Christianity. Nearly all Muslims know some of the Qur'ān by heart, since parts are recited in the daily worship, while a few memorize it in its entirety. From an early period Muslims have insisted that the Qur'ān cannot be adequately translated into other languages. Consequently, when many non-Arabs became Muslims, they had to memorize or read the Qur'ān in Arabic, and this led to a more careful study of Arabic grammar and lexicography. To establish the true meaning of words pre-Islamic poetry was collected, and for the understanding of the poetry a knowledge of legendary history was found desirable. As the number of educated persons increased, poetry continued to be written in Arabic and its scope extended, while belles-lettres were cultivated, especially the miscellany. Out of the Arab love of language there grew the *maqāma* (inadequately translated as 'assembly'), a sophisticated literary form with elaborate word play. All these constitute the Arabic humanities. Round them there was some organization of higher education as early as the beginning of the ninth century, and by the end of the eleventh century university-type institutions had been established in most of the chief cities. Teaching has been going on continuously for a thousand years in the university-mosque of Al-Az'har in Cairo.

In addition to the disciplines mentioned the Muslims came to cultivate what they described as the 'foreign sciences', namely, Greek philosophy, medicine, astronomy and the like. At the time of the Arab conquest of Iraq these were being studied and taught in Christian schools there, and many of the standard Greek works had been translated into Syriac, the medium of instruction. Translation of these books into Arabic began before 800 but was first properly organized by the caliph al-Ma'mūn (813–33). For a time Greek learning was cultivated chiefly in the Christian medical schools, but in the tenth century original works began to come from Muslims – or perhaps we should say 'nominal Muslims', since they were usually regarded as heretics, and their work came only gradually into the main stream of Islamic thinking. For the moment this may suffice as an account of the 'foreign sciences', since more will have to be said later.

Islamic culture may be said to have come of age about the middle of the tenth century, and it remained at a high level at least until the seventeenth century. It was not restricted to any one region of the Islamic empire, but was widely spread wherever Islam was strong. Scholars travelled far afield to have personal contact with the most celebrated teachers. Though Umayyad Spain did not recognize the ʿAbbāsid caliph in Baghdad, it remained in cultural contact with the Islamic east. From Spain it was easy to travel to intellectual centres like Medina, Damascus and Baghdad. Important books found their way to Spain within a few years of their publication in the east, while the scholars and writers of Islamic Spain made notable contributions to Arabic literature and learning. Such was the culture in which proleptically Spain was immersed when the Arabs and Berbers conquered it in the early eighth century.

Islamic presence and European response

The invasions of Spain and Sicily meant that for a time there was an Islamic presence on the fringes of Latin Christendom. This presence, however, was not in itself an urgent matter which demanded a vigorous response except from the immediate neighbours of the Muslims. The crusading movement of the later eleventh century may be regarded as a vigorous response to Islam, but its centre was in northern France, far from direct contact with the Muslim states. If it is correct to assume that the crusading movement was a response to Islam, we are constrained to ask how it was that Islam came to be felt as a threat at so great a distance from its actual presence.

Apart from the mercantile contacts to be noticed in the next lecture, there was a certain amount of coming and going between France and Spain. Among the French there was presumably still some memory of the victory of Charles Martel in 732 and of the campaigns of Charlemagne, even if the episode which is at the centre of the *Song of Roland* (*Chanson de Roland*) did not receive its later interpretation until the eleventh century. Charlemagne was in diplomatic relations with the caliph of Baghdad, Hārūn ar-Rashīd, as well as with the latter's enemy, the Umayyad emir of Spain; and by this channel some knowledge of the vastness and power of the Islamic world might have reached Europe. In 858 two monks of Saint Germain des Prés were sent to Spain to collect the remains of St Vincent of Saragossa and bring them back to Paris; when they discovered that these had disappeared, they were encouraged to proceed to Cordova, and there received the remains of three martyrs executed in 852 for shouting insults against Islam in the mosque.[9] While they were in Cordova they presumably gained some information about Islam and the condition of Christians under Muslim rule. Central Italy was also directly affected through much of the ninth century. As already noted, Rome itself was threatened, and about 880 the Pope was making annual payments to obtain security from attacks. Some knowledge of Rome's difficulties presumably passed to Christian leaders elsewhere. None of this explains why men in the north of France, in Flanders and in Germany should have been so vehement in their hostility to Muslims, but these details may have contributed to the formation of a picture of Islam as the great enemy.

A closer connection with parts of France came about through the growth of the pilgrimage to Compostela.[10] Shortly before the middle of the ninth century a Roman sarcophagus was found, and the legend spread that it contained the bones of St James, brought thither from Palestine. Pilgrims began to come, at first doubtless only from Galicia; but in course of time the fame of the shrine spread and many pilgrims came from north of the Pyrenees. The first name recorded is that of a French bishop who made the pilgrimage in 951 with a large party. The pilgrimage was encouraged by the monks of Cluny, and a regular pilgrim route established with hospices where the pilgrims could receive food and lodging. In medieval Spanish texts this is actually known as *camino francés*, the French way, though it must have been used by German and Italian pilgrims as well as French. In 997 Santiago was attacked and plundered by Almanzor, but the tomb itself was not violated. This is a sign of the wealth and importance of the shrine by this date. In the present context it is also to be inferred that knowledge of the position of Christians in Spain and of their struggle against the Muslims must have travelled northwards along the pilgrim route. As will be seen later, this eventually led to Frenchmen and others participating in the Reconquista. For the moment the point to be emphasized is that the Islamic presence in Spain and Sicily had repercussions in more northerly regions.

TWO

COMMERCE AND TECHNOLOGY

The place of trade in Islamic lands

The Islamic or Arab presence in Spain and Sicily from the eighth century onwards and the European presence in the Levant during the Crusading period would in themselves have led to a certain sharing of culture, or – to be more precise – to the adoption by western Europeans of many features of Islamic culture. This spread of Islamic culture, however, was undoubtedly fostered by the skill and energy of the Arabs in the field of trade and commerce. Not merely was there a relatively homogeneous culture throughout the lands under Muslim domination, but the goods produced by Muslims were carried far beyond the frontiers of the Islamic lands.

Trade has indeed been a feature of human societies from an early stage in their development, but it has always had a special place in Islamic civilization. The religion of Islam was first and foremost a religion of traders, not a religion of the desert and not a religion of peasants. The idea that the austere monotheism of Islam was associated with man's experience of his own insignificance in vast desert solitudes was popularized in the nineteenth century by Ernest Renan and others, but it has little foundation in fact. The first Muslims were not bedouin actually living in the desert, but men from the commercial centre of Mecca and the agricultural oasis of Medina. It is true, of course, that the manpower for the great Arab expansion came mainly from the desert; and it might also be said that Islamic morality incorporates the great virtues of the desert, though in a form suited to urban life. Similarly the desert was the medium across which the merchants of Mecca conducted their commercial operations, just as the sea was the medium of Venetian and other Italian traders. On the other hand, the bedouin have seldom been devout Muslims, either in Muḥammad's day or in later times.

Again, though there are now many millions of Muslim peasants, the Islamic religion, far from being closely associated with their agricultural activities (as are the religions of other peasant communities), neglects and discourages them. One mark of this is the fact that Islam has adopted a calendar of twelve lunar months or 354 days, and has rejected intercalation or any other method of making its year correspond with the solar year and the seasons. Such a calendar is useless to the peasant. The fact that dates and cereals were grown in the oasis of Medina has left little trace on the religious outlook of early Islam.

In contrast to this lack of concern for the bedouin and the peasants, the Islamic religion has always produced an atmosphere favourable to trade. Mecca, where it first appeared, was a town of commerce and high finance, for the great merchants of Mecca organized commerce and small industries in the region from southern Palestine to south-west Arabia, with extensions into Africa. In later times, while Islam has often spread through social pressures following on military conquest, there are parts of the world, such as East and West Africa and South-east Asia, where conversions to Islam have come about mainly through the activities of businessmen. These, while in pagan areas, have made no secret about engaging in worship five times a day. Their sincerity and their serene assumption of the superiority of Islam have impressed the pagans with whom they had business relations. Conversions together with intermarriage have led to the formation of small Muslim communities in pagan areas and these have gradually grown.[1] Thus throughout the Islamic world conditions generally favoured commercial activity. Travel was easy, at least for Muslims. It has been suggested that the whole was a single free-trade area, and this may well be true, though it should not be assumed that the volume was everywhere the same. It seems clear, however, that trade flourished in most Islamic regions and led to a notable similarity in material culture.

When Spain and Sicily came under Muslim rule, they were at once in commercial relationships with other Islamic regions and gradually adopted the externals of Islamic civilization. The assimilation of Islamic culture came about naturally. The Arabs of Spain, for example, wanted the material luxuries to which they had been accustomed in Damascus; and the local inhabitants, since they admired the Arabs, wanted to share as far as possible in the external aspects of their life. A similar process was to be seen in European colonies in the nineteenth century. In Spain and Sicily the result was that the Islamic presence was not only military and political but also cultural.

Trade between western Europe and the Islamic world[2]

When one comes to consider the precise form of the trade between western Europe and the Islamic world, there are many obscurities, but a brief sketch of some salient points will suffice for present purposes. Henri Pirenne argued that the Arab conquest of North Africa and Spain altered old patterns of trade and caused western Europe to look northwards rather than to the Mediterranean.[3] Though Spain was in contact with the eastern Mediterranean, in most of western Europe trade was at a low ebb in the later eighth century, and it was only gradually that trade between Arabs and Europeans developed. The Arabs appear to have been the active agents in promoting this trade. By about 800 most of the Mediterranean was dominated by their fleets, though the Byzantines maintained themselves in the Adriatic and Aegean. Arab pirates had bases on Sardinia and Corsica until the eleventh century, while from 891 to 973 there was a centre at Fraxinetum (Garde-Freinet) on the coast between Marseilles and Nice from which both maritime and overland raids set out.[4] On occasion the so-called 'pirates' may have attacked Muslim ships, but they probably contributed greatly to Arab command of the seas. As a result Arabs are heard of at Amalfi, which was often their ally, from the ninth century onwards, and at Pisa from the tenth. There is even some slight evidence for contacts of this kind in the eighth century.

By the second half of the tenth century trade between western Europe and the Islamic world was developing in a definite pattern, and its volume was increasing. The most noteworthy feature was that the actual transporting of goods across the Mediterranean had come to be in the hands of the Italians and not of the Arabs. Amalfi and Venice had first found the route across the Mediterranean not merely to Tunisia but also to Egypt and Syria. They were soon followed by Pisa and Genoa, and these soon ousted Amalfi, perhaps because they were more convenient ports for goods from the north. Even in the transport of goods from the Maghrib or Islamic west (Spain and North Africa) to the east the Arabs seem to have played less part than Maghribi Jews.

The reasons for the decline of the Arab share of the carrying trade are obscure. Claude Cahen has argued plausibly that it cannot have been due to Arab unwillingness to travel in non-Muslim lands nor to the exclusion of Muslims by the rulers of these lands, but rather to Arab lack of interest in trade with Europe (apart from Italy and the Byzantine empire); they may have thought that the volume of trade was too slight for their attention, or they may have found that better results were obtained when the transport of goods was left in non-Muslim hands. The decisions were not altogether in the hands of the Arab merchants, however, for Fāṭimid Egypt and probably other Islamic governments made the foreign trader come to their own markets and pay taxes there. Thus goods were carried between Italy and Egypt by Italians, but the Italians were not allowed to pass through Egypt to the Red Sea or the Sudan. The Italians seem to have adopted the same principle in their dealings with central Europe, and the basis of Byzantine practice was similar. Such a fiscal policy was more in the interests of the governments than of the merchants, and is an indication that, though Islam was favourable to trade, Muslim merchants had little political power.

About the year 1000 changes seem to have taken place in the volume of trade along different routes. Some of these are connected with the growth of Fāṭimid power. The Fāṭimids, a Shīʿite dynasty which rejected the claims of the ʿAbbāsid caliphs in Baghdad, had established themselves in Tunisia in 909, and then in 969 had conquered Egypt, moved the seat of their government there, and founded Cairo as their capital. Because of expansionist aims the Fāṭimids wanted either wood for ships or complete ships, and they needed iron from Italy and other parts of Europe. The Italian merchants who had traded with them in Tunisia were encouraged to go straight to Egypt. East of Suez also the pattern of trade changed in favour of the Fāṭimids. Navigation seems to have become difficult in the Persian gulf, probably because a body of revolutionaries, the Qarmaṭians (Carmathians), had seized power in Bahrein. Because of this, goods from India, south-east Asia and China went instead to the Red Sea, either to the Yemen or to Egypt. Relations also declined between eastern Europe and central Asia, and caravans from Iraq and Persia, instead of going to Constantinople or northern Syria, were encouraged to make for Alexandria or Tripoli; the latter, with much of Syria, was in Fāṭimid hands.

In its specific character this trade between western Europe and the Islamic world bore some resemblance to the 'colonial trade' of the nineteenth and twentieth centuries, except that Europe was in the position of colony. Its imports from the Islamic world consisted mainly of consumer goods, and in return it exported raw materials and slaves. Many of the latter came from the pagan Slav peoples; and it is because of this that in English, French and other European languages, and also in Arabic, the word for 'slave' is a derivative of 'Slav'. Much of the trade in slaves was through Spain, but the slaves proceeded to Egypt and further east. The conversion of the Slavs to Christianity in the eleventh century led to a drying up of this source of supply. Among important raw materials, as already noted, were timber for ships and iron, since these were scarce in Islamic lands. By the twelfth century or earlier Europe is found in one minor respect obtaining raw material from the Arabs. The European textile industry employed methods which required alum, and the supply of this commodity was obtained from Egypt, although alum was not much used by Egyptian industry.

Techniques connected with sea-faring[5]

Commercial activity is in a sense the mechanism by which a sharing of material culture is brought about. This sharing may be observed in many spheres, not least in techniques connected with shipbuilding and seafaring, which are directly relevant to the trading activities which have been described.

In respect of the rig of ships the Arabs brought to the Mediterranean the fruits of their experience in the Indian Ocean, where they came to dominate the extensive trade in the vast semicircle from Kilwa in East Africa to the Straits of Malacca and beyond. It was in the Indian Ocean that the lateen sail, despite its western name, was invented, and into the Mediterranean the Arabs introduced the lateen caravel. The advantage of such ships was that they could beat against the wind, whereas the square-rigged carracks of the Mediterranean could only sail before the wind. The principle of the lateen sail was adopted by European shipbuilders and further developed; and this eventually made possible the construction of the larger ships which were capable of crossing the Atlantic and undertaking the other great voyages of discovery. The most important advances were those made between 1440 and 1490 by Portuguese and Spanish shipwrights. The number of masts was increased and then the number of sails. A mixed rig was employed, with a square-sail on the fore-mast and lateen sails on the main mast and mizen. In this way a sufficient area of sail was obtained to propel relatively large ships.

The main steps in the development of the mariner's compass seem to have been shared between the Arabs and the Europeans. The details are obscure, but there are clearly many stages between discovering the property of a magnetized piece of iron and producing a serviceable instrument for navigation. The first step was probably to place a 'needle' or magnetized piece of iron on a small piece of wood floating in water; but many further steps were clearly needed. It was supposed for a time that the Chinese had invented the compass in the third millennium B.C., but this was due to the misunderstanding of a legend. The first record of the use of the compass by Chinese sailors is dated about 1100 A.D., and it is also said that they originally observed its use by foreigners. The latter might well be Arabs, since the Chinese were trading in the Persian Gulf and the Red Sea by the ninth century A.D. When Europeans came into contact with Chinese mariners, they found that the compass these used was inferior to their own; but the historian of the voyages of Vasco da Gama considered that the Arabs they met in the Indian Ocean were hardly inferior to the Portuguese in their maritime skills.

Another report ascribes the invention of the compass to Flavio Gioia of Amalfi in 1302. This report cannot be accepted exactly as it stands, for in European literature there are references to the compass in 1187 and 1206. In Arabic literature it is mentioned about 1220, probably as being used in eastern waters, and its use on a voyage from Tripoli to Alexandria is recorded in 1242. It is probable, then, that Gioia was responsible for some refinement, perhaps the addition of a card with the points of the compass marked. From these facts, despite their obscurity, it seems reasonably certain that the Arabs and the western Europeans were sharing their technical knowledge in this matter. The basic development may well have been the work of the Arabs, but some of the later refinements were certainly due to the Europeans.

In other minor ways also the Arabs contributed to European techniques of seafaring. The portolans or nautical charts, which were an important tool of the navigator, were developed by the Genoese and others from Islamic cartography. Evidence of a general kind is provided by the adoption of Arabic words in European languages. In English the most notable are: admiral, cable, shallop or sloop, barque, monsoon; but other languages have rather more.

In this connection it may be noted that it was from the Arabs that Europeans gained a wider and more precise geographical knowledge. In the early twelfth century, to judge from the writing of William of Malmesbury, men still thought that the whole world apart from Europe belonged to the Muslims. By about the middle of that century, however, relatively accurate knowledge of India, China and the northern half of Africa was made accessible to Europeans through the initiative of two kings of Sicily, Roger II (1127–54) and his son William I (1154–66). Under their patronage an Arab scholar from North Africa and Cordova, al-Idrīsī (1100–66), produced a complete description of the world as then known to the Muslims. He had studied previous Arab geographers, had extracted information by the king's authority from visitors to Sicily, and had himself travelled extensively from Asia to the west coast of England. What he had learned he set out in a series of seventy maps (ten for each of the seven climes), accompanied by written descriptions comprising what is sometimes known as 'the Book of Roger'.[6]

Agricultural products and minerals[7]

The Arabs are not usually associated with the advancement of agriculture. Islamic systems of land tenure, in combination with the Islamic law of inheritance which led to the fragmentation of estates, and the practice of establishing *awqāf* or religious trusts, controlled by lawyers, discouraged the owners of land from themselves making improvements and inducing the cultivators to adopt superior methods. Nevertheless there was a relatively prosperous agriculture in most of the Islamic lands where agriculture was possible. Because of this the Arabs were able to raise the level of agriculture in a country like Spain.

The rainfall in Spain, apart from the north, is slight, and without irrigation many forms of agriculture are impossible. There was irrigation in both Roman and Visigothic Spain, but it is virtually certain that the Arabs improved and extended this on the basis of what they had learned in the Middle East about ways of conserving and distributing water. Evidence for this is the large number of Spanish words pertaining to irrigation techniques which have been derived from Arabic, especially the following: *acequia*, irrigation ditch; *alberca*, artificial pool; *aljibe*, cistern; *noria*, irrigating wheel or draw well; *arcaduz*, water conduit or bucket; *azuda*, Persian wheel; *almatriche*, canal; *alcantarilla*, bridge, sewer; *atarjea*, small drain; *atanor*, water pipe; *alcorque*, hollow round the base of a tree to hold water. Besides this evidence from language there is a great similarity between the actual forms of wheels still used in Spain and those found in the Middle East and Morocco; and it is most likely that such wheels were invented in the Middle East.[8]

With the development of irrigation went the introduction into Spain of plants which can only be grown where there is adequate water. Among these were: sugar-cane, rice, oranges, lemons, aubergines, artichokes, apricots and cotton. For all these even the English words came originally from Arabic. The cultivation of plants already known in Spain was of course continued and developed. Apart from cereals there were grapes, olives and figs; there were also cherries, apples, pears, pomegranates and almonds. In the warmer districts there were bananas and palms. There were many plants used for flavouring and colouring, such as saffron, carthamus or bastard saffron, cumin, coriander, henna, woad and madder. Where there were sufficient mulberry trees, a silk industry flourished. Flax was cultivated and linen exported, while the esparto grass which grew wild on steppe lands was collected and made into articles of various kinds.

The mineral wealth of Spain was more fully exploited than in earlier times. Spanish iron and copper were widely known and esteemed, as was also the cinnabar from which mercury was extracted. There are reports of the production of gold, silver, tin and lead. Precious and semi-precious stones were sought and collected.

The arts of 'gracious living'

This wide variety of materials from agriculture and mining was used by the Arabs of Spain to enhance the pleasure of life, at least for the well-to-do; but even the poorer classes had some share in the good things of Islamic Spain. The modern tourist, entranced by the beauty of the Alcázar of Seville or the Alhambra, surmises something of the luxurious life of those who once lived there; and the student of literature gains further glimpses of this style of 'gracious living' from anecdotes and poems.

Not surprisingly there were in Islamic Spain various industries producing luxury goods both for the home market and for export. Among the products were gorgeous textiles in woollens, linens and silks, of which a few specimens are still preserved. Furs of many kinds were to be had in Spain, and these were used to trim garments or as separate articles of apparel. The ceramic industry was highly developed, and techniques such as the painting of tiles were introduced from the east. The secret of manufacturing crystal was discovered in Cordova in the second half of the ninth century. There were many skilled craftsmen in fine metal work who produced elaborate vessels or shapes of animals in brass and bronze, and inlaid these with silver and gold. By the tenth century Cordova had become the rival of Byzantium in the arts of the goldsmith, the silversmith and the jeweller. Marvellous necklaces, bracelets, earrings and other ornaments have survived to enable us to appreciate the high level of technical and artistic attainment. The same is true of the carving of ivory. Wood also was carved and was inlaid with ivory and mother-of-pearl. There were many forms of decorative leather-work, not least in book-binding.

The framework of this life of luxury was constituted by the glorious buildings which we call 'Moorish'. In these some use was made of local materials and previous Iberian techniques; even the horse-shoe arch, that distinctive feature of the Moorish style of architecture, was apparently taken over from Visigothic buildings. Yet the evidence of the Spanish language suggests that it was chiefly the Arabs who were responsible for many improvements and refinements in building techniques. The words for 'architect' and 'mason' are from Arabic, *alarife* and *albañil*. So also are the following: *alcázar*, castle; *alcoba*, bedroom; *azulejo*, tile; *azotea*, roof terrace; *baldosa*, fine paving tile; *zaguán*, vestibule; *aldaba*, door-knocker; *alféizar*, window-sill; *falleba*, lock for doors or windows. It is reported that Byzantine craftsmen were brought to Spain, but there appear to be more elements of Syrian than of Byzantine inspiration, so that Arab craftsmen from the east may also have worked in Spain.[9]

Before these various elements could be brought together to constitute a genuinely gracious style of life, a high standard of taste had to be formed throughout the upper layers of society. Here the influence of such eastern centres as Medina and Baghdad was important. A leading part in disseminating this influence was played by a musician and singer called Ziryāb, who lived in Cordova from 822 until his death in 857.[10] As a youth he had sung and played in Baghdad before Hārūn ar-Rashīd (786–809). After he had decided to leave Baghdad he was enticed to Cordova by the Umayyad rulers and given lavish presents. He not merely raised the level of playing and singing, but became an arbiter of fashion and taste in general of the calibre of Petronius and Beau Brummell. Thus he is said to have introduced an order in which different dishes were to be served at a banquet; and it seems likely that the order of courses we ourselves follow on the most formal occasions goes back to Ziryāb. He was also concerned with the preparation of the different dishes and brought many recipes from the east. He showed people that fine glassware could be more elegant than gold and silver goblets. He paid attention to hairdressing and other forms of beauty culture. And he made it a standard practice to wear clothes of different kinds in the different seasons of the year. Such ideas came to be widely accepted among the upper classes in Moorish Spain.

Ziryāb was only one of many musicians. The Arabs invented or improved many different types of instrument. Specially popular in the east were songs accompanied by the lute, pandore, psaltery, flute or the like, while drums and tambourines were used to strengthen the rhythm. Instrumental music was sometimes played on military occasions, and was a regular part of the worship of some mystical fraternities with a view to inducing ecstasy. There are many Arabic books on musical theory, some based on Greek writers, some making fresh advances. In both the theory and practice of music the Arabs of Spain took their full share. Seville was noted for the production of musical instruments; and the Arabic names of the lute, guitar, rebec and naker suggest that these came to Europe from the Arabs. A few works on theory were translated into Latin or Hebrew, but these had less influence in Europe than Arab practice – the actual singing and playing – which was spread by minstrels.[11] The Morris dancers of England – the word is a corruption of 'Moorish' dancers – perform with a hobby-horse and bells and are reminiscent of the Arab minstrels.

One part of 'gracious living' was familiarity with books, and for the Arabs the possession of books was made easier by the use of paper. Paper was invented in China, and it is said that at the middle of the eighth century some Chinese craftsmen made prisoners by the Arabs earned their freedom by producing paper. Its importance was soon perceived, since it was much cheaper than the main alternative, Egyptian papyrus. Hārūn ar-Rashīd's vizier, Yaḥyā the Barmakid, built the first paper-mill in Baghdad about the year 800. The manufacture of paper then spread westwards through Syria and North Africa to Spain, and it came into common use. In the twelfth century pilgrims from France to Compostela took back pieces of paper as a great curiosity, though Roger II of Sicily had used paper for a document in 1090. From Spain and Sicily the use of paper spread into western Europe, but paper-mills were not established in Italy and Germany until the fourteenth century.

The 'gracious living' of the Arabs of Spain was essentially urban living and presupposes the existence of cities where law and order is preserved and numbers of people live together in peace. It is therefore not surprising to find that Spanish has a number of words of Arabic origin dealing with municipal administration and the control of commercial activity.[12] Among administrative officials are the *alcalde* (mayor), the *alcaide* (governor of a fortress), and the *zalmedina* (magistrate). The market was the *zoco* or *azoguejo* or else, if for grain, the *alhóndiga*. A warehouse was *almacen* and the customshouse *aduana*, while a public sale was *almoneda*. Many words for weights and measures were from Arabic, and the man who inspected these was *zabazoque* (literally, chief of the market) or *almotacén*; the taxes were collected by *almojarife*. In this sphere of municipal administration the practice of Islamic Spain was founded on ideas derived from the Middle East where the Arabs had entered into the heritage of thousands of years of experience of urban living.

The mingling of cultures in Moorish Spain

One school of historians of Spain has strongly insisted that there never ceased to exist in north-west Spain a body of Christians who had maintained from Visigothic times a relatively self-contained and essentially Christian culture, and that in course of time they took over certain articles and practices from the Muslims and at the same time borrowed the Arabic word. This suffices, it is held, to explain the presence of Arab features in Spanish life and words of Arabic derivation in the Spanish language. A more likely view is that no such Christian enclave maintained itself in strict isolation in the north-west, but that in most of Islamic Spain there was gradually formed a homogeneous Hispano-Arabic culture which eventually permeated the north-west and dominated the local culture.[13] In the Islamic lands both Christians and Muslims were apparently familiar with Arabic, though for the purposes of daily life both used a Romance dialect with a partly arabized vocabulary. The Christians under Muslim rule were so closely identified with the culture of the rulers in everything except religion that they came to be known as Mozarabs or 'arabizers'. In a much-quoted passage written in 854 Bishop Alvar complains that the young men of the Christian community are so attracted by Arabic poetry that they have abandoned the study of Latin for that of Arabic.[14] The Jews, whose position had been improved by the Arab invaders, also accepted the dominant culture in everything except religion. Although this dominant culture was basically Islamic in inspiration, the Islamic or Arab elements in it were fused with Iberian elements.[15] Symbolic of this is the adoption of the horse-shoe arch from the Visigoths.

The spread of this Hispano-Arab culture was encouraged in two ways by the Reconquista. Firstly, some of the Christian princes persuaded numbers of Mozarabs to leave the south and settle in the uninhabited and disputed territory of the marches. Secondly, as the area under Christian rule came to include Islamic towns many of the Muslim inhabitants continued to live there under the Christians. The town remained essentially Islamic or Hispano-Arab in culture, and it was the immigrant conquerors who tended to change. An outstanding example of this is Toledo which was reconquered in 1085 and thereafter played an important part in the intellectual history of Europe.

The spread of Islamic culture into Europe

There have been many discussions of the relationship of Arabic and European elements in the sphere of poetry, notably in respect of Provençal poetry and the troubadours.[16] To Hispano-Arabic culture the Iberians contributed the idea of the strophic form in poetry, for classical Arabic poetry consists of 'odes', sometimes containing over a hundred verses, in which each verse has the same metrical form and the same rhyme. When Moorish Spain had brought the strophic forms of the *muwashshaḥ* and the *zajal* to a high level of artistry, they were adopted in the east also. The homogeneity of the culture is further shown by the close similarity of the Arabic *zajal* with the Romance *villancico*, a similarity which amounts to virtual identity. The existence of a homogeneous culture in Moorish Spain enables us to understand the similarities and coincidences between Provençal poetry and the court poetry in Arabic, even though we cannot give a full explanation and say precisely where particular features originated. Both the court poetry of Spain and that of Provence had underlying them a popular poetry whose existence is attested, though hardly anything of it has survived; and it was this popular poetry which formed the connecting link between Spain and Provence, since singers moved backwards and forwards between Muslim and Christian territories.

The attraction of Arabic culture for Christians is further exemplified by the life of the Sicilian court, especially under Roger II and Frederick II. These kings lived in luxurious surroundings comparable to those of Cordova, and adopted the dress of the Arabs and much else of their outward manner of life. The suggestion that Frederick kept a harem is almost certainly a slander, though he certainly employed dancing-girls and singing-girls. Arabic poetry was cultivated at the court, and through the popular poetry derived from this may have moulded early Italian poetry. The kings had Muslims as officials and counsellors, and patronized scholars from Syria and Baghdad. Frederick in particular encouraged scientific and philosophical discussions at his court; and it was for him that Michael Scot made some translations into Latin.

This refinement of life gradually spread northwards from Spain and Sicily. The experiences of the Crusaders in Islamic lands doubtless contributed something to the spread of Arab culture in western Europe, but very little can be pinpointed. How 'gracious living' in the Arab manner had spread to Pisa may be seen in the Chronicle of Fra Salimbene where he describes the impression made on him by a brief visit to the house of a wealthy merchant there.

> 'Going begging for bread with our baskets we happened on a cortile which we entered. And there was a leafy vine spread out overhead. Its verdure was delightful to behold and it was a pleasure to rest beneath its shade. There were leopards and many strange beasts from across the seas.... And there were youths and maidens in the flower of their youth, richly dressed and of charming countenance. They held in their hands violins, viols, zithers and other instruments with which they made melody, accompanying the music with appropriate gestures. No one there moved, no one spoke, all listened in silence. And the song was so new and so delightful, both on account of the words and the variety of voices and the manner of singing that it filled the heart with joyousness. No one spoke to us. We said nothing to them. And the music of the voices and the instruments never

ceased all the time we stayed there, and we remained there a long time and knew not how to go away. I know not (God knows) whence came such a vision of so much delight, for never before had I seen anything like it, nor has it been granted to me since ever to see it again.'[17]

Thus through trade contacts and through political presence in Spain and Sicily the superior culture of the Arabs gradually made its way into western Europe. Though western Europe was in contact with the Byzantine empire it took over far more from the Arabs than from the Byzantines – a further reason for thinking that the contribution of the Crusades to cultural diffusion was a minor one. Three points may be made in conclusion: first, the contributions of the Arabs to western Europe were chiefly in respect of matters which tended to the refinement of life and the improvement of its material basis; second, most Europeans had little awareness of the Arab and Islamic character of what they were adopting; third, the 'gracious living' of the Arabs and the literature that accompanied it stimulated the imagination of Europe and not least the poetic genius of the Romance peoples.

THREE

ARAB ACHIEVEMENTS IN SCIENCE AND PHILOSOPHY

In speaking of Arab achievements in science and philosophy the important question to ask is: how far were the Arabs mere transmitters of what the Greeks had discovered and how far did they make original contributions? Many European scholars seem to approach the subject with some prejudice against the Arabs. Even some of those who praise them do so grudgingly. The writer of the chapter on 'Astronomy and Mathematics' in *The Legacy of Islam* (Baron Carra de Vaux) felt compelled to begin by disparaging the Arabs.

> 'We must not expect to find among the Arabs the same powerful genius, the same gift of scientific imagination, the same "enthusiasm", the same originality of thought that we have among the Greeks. The Arabs are before all else the pupils of the Greeks; their science is a continuation of Greek science which it preserves, cultivates, and on a number of points develops and perfects.'

A moment later, however, he goes on to elaborate this last phrase and concedes that

> 'the Arabs have really achieved great things in science; they taught the use of ciphers (*sc.* Arabic numerals), although they did not invent them, and thus became the founders of the arithmetic of everyday life; they made algebra an exact science and developed it considerably and laid the foundations of analytical geometry; they were indisputably the founders of plane and spherical trigonometry which, properly speaking, did not exist among the Greeks. In astronomy they made a number of valuable observations.'

It is clearly difficult to give a balanced assessment of the scientific achievements of the Arabs. When one becomes aware of the prejudice against them – which is doubtless linked with the distorted image of Islam to be discussed in a later lecture – one tends to exaggerate what they actually did. In what follows I shall be as objective as I can. I shall consider the main sciences separately, and with regard to each I shall ask both what was the general Arab or Muslim contribution and what was the specific contribution of the Arabs of Spain. Before launching into this detailed examination of the sciences, however, I must say something about the translation of Greek scientific and philosophical works into Arabic.[1]

When Iraq, Syria and Egypt were conquered by the Arabs in the seventh century, Greek science and philosophy were cultivated in various centres. There was a famous school at Alexandria in Egypt, but it was moved first to Syria, and then about 900 to Baghdad; there the members of the school, though Christians, shared fully in philosophical discussions. At Ḥarrān in northern Mesopotamia there was a school of the semi-philosophical sect known as the Ṣābi'ans; its members also gravitated towards Baghdad. The most important centre, however, was the Nestorian Christian college of Gondēshāpūr, which was specially famous for its medical teaching. From this college came the court physicians of Hārūn ar-Rashīd and his successors for over a hundred years. As a result of contacts such as this the caliphs and other leading Muslims became aware of what was to be learned from Greek science, and arranged for important books to be translated into Arabic from Syriac (the language of instruction at Gondēshāpūr and elsewhere). A few translations appear to have been made in the eighth century, but the work of translating began seriously only in the reign of al-Ma'mūn (813–33), who founded an institution mainly for this purpose, 'the House of Wisdom' (*bayt al-ḥikma*).

From this time onwards there was a great flood of translations which continued throughout the ninth and for most of the tenth century until everything available in Greek which was of interest to the Arabs had been translated. The first translations were made from Syriac, because a large number of Greek works had already been translated into that language for the sake of the Syriac-speaking Christians. It was also easier to find men who knew both Syriac and Arabic, for Syriac was widely spoken in Iraq whereas a knowledge of Greek was rare. In course of time, however, translations came to be made directly from Greek into Arabic. The adoption of this superior method is attributed mainly to the most famous of all the translators, a Nestorian Christian from Hira called Ḥunayn ibn-Is'ḥāq (809–73). He was well versed in all the knowledge of his time but especially in medicine, becoming court physician to the caliph al-Mutawakkil (*regnabat* 847–61) and a teacher of medicine in Baghdad. He had learnt Greek and had travelled in parts of the Byzantine empire collecting manuscripts of scientific and philosophical works. He was thus excellently equipped to undertake the further organization of translation. Eventually he had working with him a team of translators which included his son Is'ḥāq, his nephew Ḥubaysh and other young scholars. Among the translations ascribed to Ḥunayn are a large number of the medical works of Hippocrates and Galen, as well as the *Republic*, *Laws* and *Timaeus* of Plato, logical works of Aristotle, and mathematical works of Euclid, Archimedes and others. It may be that some of these are the production of the team rather than of Ḥunayn himself. With the work of this team translation reached its highest point, technically and linguistically, for Ḥunayn understood the value of collating manuscripts before setting out to make or revise a translation.

One of the difficulties met with by translators during the ninth century was that there was little original writing in Arabic on the topics dealt with in the books they translated. Gradually, however, as independent writings appeared in Arabic on the sciences, logic and metaphysics, a technical vocabulary was developed. It then became possible to revise the earlier translations so that their arguments had greater precision and accuracy. It was only in this later phase of revising previous translations that scholars from Spain played a part. In 951 in Cordova a Christian monk, a Spanish Jew and some Arab physicians joined to revise Ḥunayn's translation of the pharmacology of Dioscorides; and additions were made some thirty years later by another Spanish Arab physician.

Mathematics and astronomy[2]

The subjects of the first Greek books to be translated were those of immediate practical interest to the Arabs, notably medicine and astronomy. Astronomy was a practical subject mainly because of the widespread belief in astrology, but also in part because it was needed in order to know the direction of Mecca which Muslims were required to face in their prayers. Mathematics also was of practical use, and it was in fact in the sphere of mathematics that the first advances were made by the Arabs.

The first important name in both mathematics and astronomy is that of al-Khwārizmī, known to the Latin scholars as Algorismus or Alghoarismus; from his name is derived the technical term 'algorism'. He worked in the *Bayt al-ḥikma* during the caliphate of al-Ma'mūn, and died some time after 846. Al-Khwārizmī produced for al-Ma'mūn an abridged form of some Indian astronomical tables which are known as the *Sindhind* (corresponding to the Sanskrit *Siddhānta*), and which had been translated into Arabic for the caliph al-Manṣūr (*regnabat* 754–75). He was also the author of a description of the inhabited part of the earth, based on the *Geography* of Ptolemy. More influential, however, were his mathematical works. One may be reckoned the foundation of algebra – and indeed the word 'algebra' is derived from its title – while another is, apart from Indian writings, the first work on arithmetic using our present decimal notation, that is, the numerals which we know as Arabic.

There are some obscurities about the origin of the ten signs for the numerals. Arabic writers refer to them as 'Indian', but no references have been found in any Arab mathematician to an Indian author or work. This is a curious fact and has led some scholars to allege that the Arabs borrowed from the Byzantines one of the two forms in which the ten signs are found. Most scholars, however, now accept the view that the ten numerals are of Indian origin. The Greeks had a sexagesimal system for fractions and other purposes, and this continued to be used by Arab astronomers. Most persons using arithmetic, however, came to realize the advantages of the Indian system with its ten signs whose value is indicated by their position.

Al-Khwārizmī and his successors worked out methods for performing arithmetically various complex mathematical operations such as finding the square root of a number. Many operations known to the Greeks were dealt with in this way. The beginning of decimal fractions is traced to a work written about 950 by a man called al-Uqlīdisī, 'the Euclidean'. Among other mathematicians whose work was translated into Latin were an-Nayrīzī or Anaritius (d. *c.* 922) and the justly famous Ibn-al-Haytham or Alhazen (d. 1039). The latter had assimilated all the work of Greek and previous Arab mathematicians and physicists, and then went on to solve further problems. Over fifty of his books and treatises have survived. The best known is *Kitāb al-manāẓir*, which was translated into Latin as *Opticae thesaurus*. In this, among many other matters, he opposes the theory of Euclid and Ptolemy that visual rays travel from the eye to the object, and maintains instead that light travels from the object to the eye. He also discussed what is still known as 'Alhazen's problem' and gave a solution in which he solved an equation of the fourth degree. He conducted numerous experiments, and as a result of his work with spherical and parabolic mirrors and in respect of the refraction of light in passing through a transparent medium was able to give a calculation for the height of the earth's atmosphere, and almost discovered the principle of the magnifying lens.

Astronomy had been practised in Iraq for a century or more before the Arab conquest, being based partly on Greek astronomy and notably the work of Ptolemy, and partly on Indian astronomy. When the Arabs became interested in astronomy, translations were made from Sanskrit and Pahlavi as well as from Greek and Syriac. The basic theoretical text was the *Almagest* (Arabic *al-majistī*), which is the *Megalē Syntaxis* of Ptolemy. The translation, probably first made at the end of the eighth century, was several times revised, and there were many commentaries and introductions to it. Following Ptolemy the Arab astronomers believed in a fixed earth round which eight spheres revolved, carrying the sun, the moon, the five planets and the fixed stars. In order to make this system tally with the observed phenomena a complex system of epicycles and other mathematical devices was required. As time went on the Arabs were aware of the weaknesses of the Ptolemaic system and were critical of it, but they produced no satisfactory alternative, though Ibn-ash-Shāṭir of Damascus (fl. 1350) greatly simplified the mathematics.

Much of the work of the astronomers was not concerned with theory, but centred in the *zīj* or set of astronomical tables. There were many such sets of tables, and they came from Indian, Persian and Greek sources. The discrepancies between the different tables stimulated the Arabs to more accurate observations. Extremely accurate tables were produced by al-Battānī or Albategnius about 900. His exact observations of eclipses were used for comparative purposes as late as 1749.

Moorish Spain played its full part in mathematical and astronomical studies, and European scholars were thus able to come into contact with living disciplines. The earliest in this field was Maslama al-Majrīṭī (that is, from Madrid) who lived mostly in Cordova and died about 1007. In the first half of the eleventh century there were two noted mathematician-astronomers, Ibn-as-Samḥ and Ibn-aṣ-Ṣaffār, and an astrologer, Ibn-Abī-r-Rijāl or Abenragel. After that there are no distinguished names until the middle and end of the twelfth century when two important astronomers followed one another at Seville, Jābir ibn-Aflaḥ or Geber (but distinct from the alchemist Geber) and al-Biṭrūjī or Alpetragius. The former is specially noted for his work in spherical trigonometry, a discipline in which the Arabs in general made great advances. The latter, in line with the revived Aristotelianism of the period, criticized some of the theoretical conceptions of Ptolemy. After this there was little opportunity for such work in Spain, but something of the tradition continued in North Africa. Long before this, however, in the early twelfth century a Jewish mathematician in Barcelona, Abraham bar-Ḥiyya ha-Nasi, often known as Savasorda, had begun translating Arabic scientific works into Hebrew and writing original treatises in that language. These Hebrew works played an important part in the transmission to Europe of the Arabic scientific heritage.

Medicine[3]

In the realm of medicine the Arabs, on conquering Iraq, found a flourishing medical service. At the centre of this was the Nestorian Christian academy of Gondēshāpūr, which has already been mentioned. Here the study of medical theory through the standard texts of Galen and others was combined with clinical instruction in the teaching hospital associated with the academy. In the curriculum Greek science and philosophy were also included, and this combination of subjects was continued by the Muslims when they established their own schools. As a result of this it is not unusual to find men who are highly qualified in more than one field. As we shall presently see, Avicenna, though perhaps the greatest of Islamic philosophers, was also an outstanding physician; and Averroes, who was of similar calibre to Avicenna in philosophy, was at the same time a practising judge and wrote some books on medicine. The medical teaching at Gondēshāpūr was mainly based on the Greek authorities, though some use seems also to have been made of Indian writings. There was also medical teaching at Alexandria, but it was of a much inferior quality.

In Iraq the Arabs quickly realized the value of the existing medical service, and the wealthy at least among them made use of it. There are reports from early in the eighth century of medical books being translated into Arabic and hospitals founded; but the first reliable piece of information is that a hospital was established in Baghdad about 800 by a Christian physician from Gondēshāpūr called Jibrā'īl ibn-Bakhtīshūʿ. This was done on the initiative of the caliph Hārūn ar-Rashīd. It is not known whether there was another hospital in Baghdad during the ninth century, but the particulars are recorded of one founded there about 900, another in 914, two in 918 and yet another in 925. The founders were wealthy men such as viziers who gave a large sum of money as an endowment; the income from this was then used to pay the staff. In the early tenth century we also hear of doctors making medical rounds in prisons, and of arrangements for a travelling clinic and dispensary to visit the villages of lower Iraq. What Baghdad the capital began was copied in the provinces, and from the ninth century onwards hospitals were founded in the main provincial cities. One of the greatest was the Manṣūrī in Cairo, founded in 1284 in a former palace, which is said to have had accommodation for 8000 people. This hospital was lavishly appointed. Not merely were male and female patients separated, but there were separate wards for different categories such as fevers, ophthalmia, dysentery and surgical cases. Besides a number of surgeons and physicians, some of whom were specialists, there were attendants of both sexes, a large administrative staff, a dispensary, store-rooms, a chapel, a library and facilities for lecturing. When hospitals existed with this degree of sophistication, it is not surprising that there were also manuals of hospital management.

After the first period of translation, when the chief works of Galen and Hippocrates were made available in Arabic, the Christians lost their monopoly of medicine, and several Muslims reached such a stature in medical science that they stood far above their immediate predecessors and were roughly on a level with the greatest of the Greeks. They achieved this by combining vast theoretical knowledge with acute observation in the course of their clinical practice. Here it will be sufficient to mention the two most famous, Rhazes and Avicenna, and a third known to Europe as Haly Abbas; but it is worth noting the fact that for the five centuries from 800 to 1300 Arabic medical writings have been preserved from the pens of over 70 authors, mostly Muslims but also including a few Christians and Jews.

Rhazes or Abū-Bakr Muḥammad ibn-Zakariyyā' ar-Rāzī was born in 865 at Rayy near Teheran – his name means 'the man from Rayy' – and died either there or at Baghdad between 923 and 932. He was consulted about the site for a hospital in Baghdad, and is said to have been the first head of it. Above all he was a voluminous writer on all the scientific and philosophical subjects then studied, but he is generally agreed to have been best in medical science. Over fifty of his works are still extant. One of the best known is a treatise *On Small-pox and Measles* (*De la variole et de la rougeole*), which has been translated into Latin, Greek, French and English. His greatest work was *Al-Ḥāwi*, 'the Comprehensive (Book)', which was an encyclopaedia of all medical science up to that time, and had to be completed by his disciples after his death. For each disease he gave the views of Greek, Syrian, Indian, Persian and Arabic authors, and then added notes on his clinical observations and expressed a final opinion. The available sections of it were translated into Latin in the late thirteenth century by a Sicilian Jewish physician. A recent writer adds what he calls a 'human element' to his account of ar-Rāzī by mentioning the titles of some of his shorter works: *On the fact that even skilful physicians cannot heal all diseases*; *Why frightened patients forsake even the skilled physician*; *Why people prefer quacks and charlatans to skilled physicians*; *Why ignorant physicians, laymen, and women have more success than learned medical men.*

Although the excellence of the *Continens* of ar-Rāzī was widely recognized, some felt that it was too lengthy a work, and about half a century later a Persian physician set out to produce an equally comprehensive but less bulky encyclopaedia. The man was ʿAlī ibn-al-ʿAbbās al-Majūsī (d. 994), court-physician to the sultan ʿAḍud-ad-dawla, and the book was *The Complete Art of Medicine* or alternatively *Al-kunnāsh al-malakī*. It was one of the earliest medical books to be translated into Latin and proved popular, being chiefly referred to as *Liber regius*, while the author became Haly Abbas.

The second outstanding writer on medicine in Arabic was Ibn-Sīnā or Avicenna (d. 1037). Like ar-Rāzī he wrote on many subjects, and is accounted to have been greater as a philosopher than as a physician. Nevertheless his vast *Canon of Medicine* is rightly acclaimed as 'the culmination and masterpiece of Arabic systematization' (Meyerhof). It was translated into Latin in the twelfth century, and continued to dominate the teaching of medicine in Europe until the end of the sixteenth century at least. There were sixteen editions of it in the fifteenth century, one being in Hebrew, twenty editions in the sixteenth century, and several more in the seventeenth. There were also innumerable commentaries on it in Latin, Hebrew and the vernaculars.

Moorish Spain was not left behind in medical studies, although no hospital comparable to the great hospitals of the east was founded until the fourteenth century. A Jew and a Muslim from Cordova who joined in the work of translation have already been mentioned. Not long after their time appeared an original writer, Abū-l-Qāsim az-Zahrāwī (d. after 1009), known in Latin mostly as Abulcasis. His writing on surgery and surgical instruments is the outstanding Arabic contribution to this aspect of medicine. Several of the philosophers of Spain were also competent physicians. In addition to Averroes there may be named Ibn-Zuhr or Avenzoar of Seville (d. 1161) and the Jewish scholar Maimonides (d. 1204) who studied in Spain though he eventually became court-physician to Saladin in Egypt. There were still Arab doctors in Spain in the fourteenth century who wrote about the plague as they had experienced it at Granada and Almeria; they were fully aware of the contagious character of the disease.

Other sciences[4]

Of the other sciences cultivated by the Arabs the most important was alchemy in the sense of chemistry. The word 'alchemy' is applied to two rather different disciplines. One concerns itself with the allegorical and mystical interpretation of chemical changes, that is, in effect, with the spiritual development of man, and is thus far removed from what is now known as chemistry. The other discipline embraces attempts to understand the constitution of matter. This often appears to be remote from modern chemistry, because its practitioners believed in the possibility of the transmutation of the elements. When allowance is made, however, for the limited knowledge of the time, it is clear that the second type of alchemist was asking the same kind of questions as the modern chemist, and was following an experimental method that was similar in essence. Alchemical works of both types were translated into Latin, but it is only those of the scientific type which will be considered here.

In the forefront of scientific alchemy in Arabic stands a great corpus of writings attributed to a person called Jābir ibn-Ḥayyān, known in Latin as Geber, who seems to have lived in the second half of the eighth century. It is now held by scholars, however, that the writings belong to the late ninth or early tenth century. While there is much in the corpus from many branches of ancient knowledge, there is certainly a full account of alchemy as an experimental science, using various instruments and methods for treating chemical substances, and having as its basis a theory derived from Aristotelian science. The corpus describes methods for preparing many substances, and also methods for purifying them. Several words for substances and for chemical vessels have come into European languages from the Jābir corpus.

Several of the great scientific scholars of the Islamic world were expert in alchemy as in other disciplines. The physician ar-Rāzī wrote some important treatises on alchemy. The hypothesis of the transmutation of the elements was rejected by the philosopher-physician Ibn-Sīnā and by another great scholar not so far mentioned, al-Bīrūnī (d. 1048?). The latter is known mainly as an expert on India, but his studies included Indian science. In the field of alchemy he himself measured the specific gravity of many substances, attaining a high degree of accuracy.

In the fields of botany, zoology and mineralogy the work of the Arabs consisted in describing and listing the varieties of plants, animals and stones. Some of this had a practical interest in so far as these matters were connected with pharmacology and medical treatment. The best work was probably that in botany. The fundamental work, now lost, appears to have been the *Book of Plants* of a distinguished historian Abū-Ḥanīfa ad-Dīnawarī (d. 895). Most of what was important in this book was included in the extensive works of Ibn-al-Bayṭār of Malaga (d. 1248), who was primarily a pharmacologist, but made valuable contributions to botany. Some books on animals exist, but these are literary productions rather than scientific, although occasionally they contain original observations. Neither they nor the books on minerals and precious stones need be further mentioned here.

Logic and metaphysics[5]

Although medicine and astronomy first attracted the attention of the Arabs to Greek books, philosophical writings came eventually to have more influence on the main stream of Islamic thought. The Muslims were always aware of the various sciences and philosophy as 'foreign disciplines', and as such they were not included in the normal form of higher education in the Islamic world. This consisted in the religious sciences or disciplines, of which the chief was jurisprudence (*fiqh*), together with what have been called the 'Arabic humanities'. The 'foreign disciplines' were studied either in separate institutions such as schools of medicine or by informal methods. Because of this situation the average Muslim scholar knew little of Greek science apart from the philosophical ideas which had found a place in the writings of theologians such as the Muʿtazilites.

Numerous translations of Greek philosophical works were made during the ninth century, and there were probably already one or two in the eighth century. Before the actual translations were available, it is possible that theologians became familiar with Greek ideas through personal contact with men educated in the Christian medical schools. Even if the Muslims were only confronted with the Greek ideas in course of religious arguments with Christians, this would convince them of the need for having some acquaintance with Greek thought. Before long various Muslim theologians began to make use of Greek ideas in the course of their thinking. One such was Ḍirār ibn-ʿAmr who flourished in the second half of the eighth century. In these first applications of Greek ideas to Islamic dogma there was an element of trial and error, and some curious views were put forward. By the middle of the ninth century many of these hellenizing theologians had reached agreement on five basic principles and referred to themselves as 'the Muʿtazilites'. About the same time there were being written the first original philosophical works in Arabic. The writer, al-Kindī, was moreover of Arab descent.

After this first infusion of Greek ideas into Islamic theology the philosophers and the theologians went their separate ways for about two centuries. The Muʿtazilites came to be regarded as heretical, but many Sunnite theologians, following al-Ashʿarī (d. 935), accepted Muʿtazilite methods of argument and used them in defence of standard Sunnite formulations of doctrine. Meanwhile Arabic philosophy produced two men who may be reckoned among the great philosophers of the world, al-Fārābī (d. 950) and Ibn-Sīnā or Avicenna (d. 1037). These two men had worked out a philosophy which was essentially a form of Neoplatonism. In their thinking they may have received some stimulus from a work which had been translated into Arabic under the title *The Theology of Aristotle*, but which was really a version of parts of Plotinus. Al-Fārābī and Avicenna differed from Plotinus, however, in that, while he tolerated polytheism, they were strictly monotheistic, even though Sunnite doctors regarded them as heretics. One of their heresies, for example, was to believe in the eternity of the world in contradistinction from its creation in time out of nothing; this came about because they interpreted the Qur'ānic statements about creation as referring to a process of emanation by which mundane things derived their being from God.

By the eleventh century Sunnite theologians were becoming aware that they were unable to maintain their positions in arguments against the philosophers. About 1090 a brilliant young theologian, al-Ghazālī (d. 1111), by reading and private study familiarized himself with the argumentation of the Arabic Neoplatonists, wrote a lucid and objective account of their views, and then composed a devastating refutation of these. After al-Ghazālī Aristotelian logic was accepted by the more rationalist theologians as providing their methodology, but the Greek sciences were less and less cultivated. Certain types of philosophy continued to be cultivated in the east, but they had little influence on western Islam, have been little studied, and are thought by some modern scholars to be nearer to theosophy than to philosophy.

More important in the present context is the influence of Avicenna and Algazel in the west and particularly in Spain. Favourable circumstances led to the appearance there during the twelfth century of several distinguished philosophers. Ibn-Bājja or Avempace (d. 1138) at the beginning of the century was surpassed by two men towards its end, Ibn-Ṭufayl or Abubacer (d. 1185) and Ibn-Rushd or Averroes (d. 1198). Ibn-Ṭufayl's chief philosophical work, often known as the *Philosophus autodidactus*, was not known in Europe until the end of the seventeenth century, but had some influence on his younger contemporaries. Among these was the great Averroes, whom some would place above Avicenna in the list of Arab philosophers. Averroes was not a system-builder but first and foremost a great commentator on Aristotle. Despite the confusion caused by the false ascription of the so-called *Theology of Aristotle*, Averroes in his commentaries remained close to the genuine thought of the master. He thus revived an Aristotelian outlook after Arabic thought had been dominated for centuries by some form of Platonism, but he came too late to have much influence on the Islamic east. To the same philosophical milieu belonged the Arabic-writing Jewish thinker, Mūsā ibn-Maymūn or Maimonides (d. 1204), who came of a Spanish family but spent the last part of his life in Egypt.

This concludes my brief survey of Arab achievements in science and philosophy. It is unnecessary now to define more precisely the relation of the Arab contribution to the Greek and to say which was the greater. When one becomes aware of the full extent of Arab experimenting, Arab thinking and Arab writing, one sees that without the Arabs European science and philosophy would not have developed when they did. The Arabs were no mere transmitters of Greek thought, but genuine bearers, who both kept alive the disciplines they had been taught and extended their range. When about 1100 Europeans became seriously interested in the science and philosophy of their Saracen enemies, these disciplines were at their zenith; and the Europeans had to learn all they could from the Arabs before they themselves could make further advances.

FOUR

RECONQUISTA AND CRUSADE

The first lecture of this series dealt with the conquest by the Arabs of Spain and Sicily, which resulted in their being significantly present in Europe. The second lecture described how the material culture of the Arabs spread into western Europe by way of trade and how their 'gracious living' was admired and imitated. Then in the third lecture we considered the scientific and philosophical achievements of the Islamic world as a whole and noted how the Arabs of Spain shared in this aspect of Islamic intellectual life. In the remaining lectures, then, we have to consider how western Europe responded to the challenge by which it was confronted through the Arab presence on its borders; and first of all we must look at the military response, which took the form in Spain of the Reconquista and in western Europe generally of the movement of the Crusades. In the present lecture we shall look at these responses, but shall pay more attention to the underlying ideas and motives than to the actual course of events. It will be convenient, however, to commence with a brief sketch of the Reconquista.

The course of the Reconquista in Spain[1]

According to Spanish traditions some Visigothic nobles shortly after the Arab invasion withdrew to a mountainous district in the Asturias in north-west Spain, and there appointed one of their number, Pelayo, as leader. It is further claimed that, when the Muslims sent a force to break up this insurgent group, it was completely defeated by Pelayo. This series of events must be regarded as semi-legendary, though there is doubtless some underlying basis of fact. The foundation of the kingdom of the Asturias was rather the work of Alfonso I (739-57);

profiting from a Berber revolt in the north-west (about 741–2) and from the upheavals in the Arab empire which led to the fall of the Umayyad dynasty in 750, he established a small state and made it relatively secure against attack. This may be regarded as the beginning of the Reconquista.

In the north-east the Franks took advantage of the same period of troubles to recapture Narbonne (751). Under Charlemagne (768–814) there occurred the celebrated expedition against Saragossa in 778 round which has grown the *Chanson de Roland*. It appears, however, that this expedition was not part of any general strategy for advance into Spain, but an attempt to seize the opportunity given by internal Arab quarrels for extending the Frankish domains. Charlemagne's main interest was on his eastern frontiers, and his capture of Barcelona in 801 was also a relatively isolated event.

For two and a half centuries after Charlemagne the military situation was more or less stabilized by the system of the Marches. The defence of the Arab state was based on the three fortresses of Saragossa, Toledo and Mérida, with each of which a March or territory was associated. Most of the country south and east of the fortresses was settled, and was ruled according to the normal principles of Islamic government. In the Marches, however, which were to the north and west of the fortresses, the degree of Arab control varied enormously both from district to district and from year to year. The Arabs frequently sent out summer-expeditions northwards to inspire fear and to inflict punishment; but the permanent control of the north was slight, and it was possible for small centres of independence to develop. These were not necessarily independent all the time, but might on occasion be forced to pay tribute to the Arab governor of the March or to the ruler in Cordova. Nevertheless they were free from detailed interference, and preserved a measure of continuity. The kingdom of the Asturias was the first of these centres of independence. It was followed by another at Leon, to the immediate south, and the two were united in 924. Pamplona is said to have gained a measure of independence in 798, and in the ninth century developed into the kingdom of Navarre. About the same time the Count of Castile asserted his independence.

For long this independence was of an intermittent or

fluctuating character. Thus ʿAbd-ar-Raḥmān III, in the last ten years before his death in 961, was acknowledged as suzerain by the king of Leon and the Asturias, the queen of Navarre and the counts of Castile and Barcelona. This suzerainty was contrary to the practice in the eastern Islamic lands where Christians who submitted became *dhimmīs* or protected minorities and ceased to bear arms. The Spanish Christian leaders, however, on taking the oath of loyalty to ʿAbd-ar-Raḥmān and promising tribute, retained their arms and even seem to have been expected to fight on his behalf. In this the Arab statesmen were realists and saw that the system of protected minorities would not work in the conditions of northern Spain. It is also to be noted in respect of these arrangements that religion and the religious law had little influence on political decisions by Muslims in Spain at least until the year 1000. On the Christian side specifically religious motives probably did not appear until the middle of the tenth century. It is known that several important Spanish families had both Christian and Muslim members.

The disintegration of Islamic Spain in the eleventh century gave the independent states of the north a chance to expand. In 1085 their efforts were crowned by the capture of Toledo. The intervention of the Almoravid and Almohad dynasties from North Africa, coupled with dissensions among the Christians, halted the Reconquista for a century. After the decline of the Almohads, however, and the union of Leon and Castile in 1230, Ferdinand III of the united kingdom was able to capture the heart of Moorish Spain by occupying Cordova in 1236 and Seville in 1248. Thereafter things changed little for two centuries until after the union of Castile and Aragon in 1479. Then the fortified towns of the Naṣrid kingdom of Granada were taken one by one, and Granada itself finally fell in 1492.

The significance of the Reconquista

A popular view among Spanish writers has been that the driving force behind the Reconquista was a continuing zeal for the Catholic faith in some of the remnants of the Visigothic kingdom. The evidence gives little support to this view. The Asturias was never strongly Catholic and was never properly subdued by the Visigoths. The first moves for the establishment of independent states came rather from the rugged spirit of mountaineers and their desire to be free from alien rule. There is nothing to show that there was deep religious feeling in the north during the eighth and ninth centuries. Certainly in the Arab state at this period Muslims, Christians and Jews seem to have mixed freely with one another and to have shared fully in a common culture. The influence of religious differences was further weakened firstly by the fact that many Muslims and Christians had relatives adhering to the other faith, and secondly by the almost universal acceptance, at least in the towns, of the dominant culture. In this culture, too, though it was in certain senses 'Islamic', we find that until the later tenth century Arab secular ideas were more prominent than specifically religious ideas. Thus men on the fringe of this culture would not think of it as essentially religious, nor of their opposition to it as religious.

The growth of religious enthusiasm among the Christians is linked with the cult of Saint James (Santiago) of Compostela and the practice of pilgrimage to his shrine. Saint James was regarded as the brother, even the twin brother of the Lord, and the cult and the pilgrimage came to incorporate something of the old Galician or Iberian belief in the Heavenly Twins.[2] Thus from the ninth century the Galicians were fully convinced that they had divine help in their wars and that, if they persevered, they would eventually be victorious. To believe that one has divine help, however, is not the same as believing that the enemy is anti-Christian; but the more one's own effort was associated with Christianity the more the name of 'Saracens', as the opponents were presumably called, would have a religious connotation. It is not clear, however, at what point the enemy came to be regarded as primarily a religious enemy.

It is reasonably clear that on the Muslim side religious enthusiasm for fighting did not appear until some time after it had appeared among the Christians. Although the original invasion of Spain and the later summer-expeditions could be regarded as Jihād, there was probably little religious zeal among the participants. Most were doubtless moved by desire for booty. While the Umayyad dynasty remained in power in Spain, it fostered something of the essentially Arab outlook of the caliphate of Damascus. Secular Arabic poetry was much admired, and a real (or even feigned) descent from an old Arabian tribe was a source of pride. Until nearly the end of the tenth century little attention was paid to the Islamic religious disciplines, apart from the study of detailed legal prescriptions which affected daily life. Thus it was the growth of Christian self-awareness and the expansion of the Christian states which led the Arabs of Spain to think of themselves as Muslims and as engaged in the defence of Islamic territory. Even to the end, however, they were not wholly united against the Christians.

The Christians also were far from being united. Yet in so far as they became more aware of themselves as Christians fighting against the enemies of Christianity, they had a reason for uniting in military operations with their fellow-Christians. They had also a new and wider conception of their own identity. They were not just men of Leon, Navarre or Castile, but were members of Catholic Christendom fighting against its enemies. Even the local kingdoms were seen as parts of this fighting Christendom. As the centuries passed, this understanding of their identity among the inhabitants of the local kingdoms was a factor contributing both to the unity of Spain and to the close association between the new Spanish identity and militant Catholicism. In this way the Reconquista did much to make Spain what it is.

Another relevant point is that the persons who became aware of themselves as Christians were persons who shared to some extent in the common Hispano-Arabic culture. The northern kingdoms admired that culture in many respects and adopted much from it. This spread of the southern culture in the north was accelerated by two other facts. First, it was at times the policy of the Christian kings to encourage Christians from the south to settle in uninhabited parts of the Marches, and gradually to include these lands in their kingdoms; and of course the Christians brought their Hispano-Arabic culture with them. Second, as the Christian frontier moved southwards, Muslim populations remained behind under Christian rule and thus increased the Hispano-Arabic culture of the northern kingdoms. As already indicated, however, few northern Spaniards or other Western Europeans realized the Islamic provenance of many elements in this culture, and so they had no difficulty in combining acceptance of the culture with opposition to the religion. In this way Spain gained a culture which had important Arabic elements, even though she came more and more to assert her Catholic identity and to deny her indebtedness to the Arabs. The view mentioned above, which connects the Reconquista with a supposed Visigothic Catholicism in the Asturias, seems not to be derived from historical facts, but to be a projection backwards of the later Catholic and anti-Saracen identity.

The growth of the idea of Crusade[3]

The Reconquista can be contrasted with the Crusades in respect of the relation between ideas and events. In the case of the former the events largely precede the idea, whereas the idea of the Crusade precedes the actual event. The contrast is perhaps not so sharp as this formulation suggests; but it is sufficient to justify our turning now to consider the growth of the idea of Crusade.

The idea of fighting on behalf of the Christian faith probably goes back at least to the emperor Constantine. Though this idea has no place in the New Testament nor in the centuries when Christians were a persecuted minority, it could perhaps be claimed that it had Old Testament precedents. In the ninth century we find Agobard of Lyons describing the meaning of the sword given by the Pope to the Emperor as 'the subjugation of barbarous nations so that they may embrace the faith and widen the frontiers of the kingdom of the faithful'. Brun of Querfurt, who was himself influenced by the monastic reform of the tenth century, asserted that the duty of the Christian king in respect of the heathen was 'to compel them to come in' by the sword. Brun lived according to his precepts, for in 1002 he abandoned his life as a hermit, and in 1009 met a martyr's death in Prussia fighting against the heathen.

Besides this emphasis on the duty of the Christian king there was some development of the conception of the Christian warrior or knight. The development had many facets, and the story is too complex to be dealt with here. Most men agreed that the Christian should play his part in a defensive war, but some hesitated about the rightness of participating in an offensive war. There were differences about the relation between fighting and preaching. The conception of the Christian knight came to be crystallized through the liturgical service for his dedication. Thus a prayer dating back to 950 speaks of him never using his sword 'to injure anyone unjustly, but always to defend the just and right'. The further development from the conception of the Christian knight to that of the Crusader was helped by the practice of going on pilgrimage, especially to the Holy Land. The journey to Jerusalem grew in popularity during the eleventh century, but a certain amount of obstruction was also experienced from the local people. Devout persons held that the true pilgrim should not carry arms, but most Christians thought that armed self-defence was permissible. Some who had been attacked by brigands had in fact defended themselves. From this it was only a small step to asserting that it was permissible to use the sword to bring the holy places under Christian control, so that infidels could no longer obstruct Christian pilgrims. This assertion further implied that the merit of fighting the infidel was similar to that of performing a pilgrimage.

That the various strands of thought were eventually woven into the single thread of the Crusading movement came about through the policy of the reforming Popes of the later eleventh century, beginning with Leo IX (1049–54).[4] The reform had many aspects. More order and stricter standards within the Church meant centralization, and constant coming and going between Rome and the various states. It was also asserted that the Church was independent of the various states and had the right to sit in judgement on their affairs and control them. The various states were linked to Rome by the use of feudal ideas. In this way the Papacy became concerned that the states of Catholic Christendom should cease fighting one another and rather direct their energies against the infidels outside and against the heretics and other opponents within. In essence, then, the duty of the Christian warrior came to be to fight against all the enemies of the Church and the Papacy.

The situation in Spain did not escape the notice of the politicians in the Curia, especially as the state of the Church there gave them some anxiety. In the case of a Christian Spanish expedition against Barbastro in 1064, Pope Alexander II declared an indulgence for all participants. In this expedition a large contingent from France took part, including Duke Guillaume of Aquitaine. It seems clear that these Frenchmen were mostly ordinary men fired with religious zeal, so that the expedition was in principle a Crusade; it was not a war in which princes fulfilled their duty of defending and extending Christendom. The papal concern for affairs in Spain continued. In a letter addressed to various counts and knights of Catalonia and probably dated shortly after the preaching of the Crusade at Clermont, Urban II promised that those who fell in an expedition to help Tarragona would have the same privileges as those who went east, and called on these particular men rather to undertake the task nearer home.

Encouragement was also given by the Popes to other enterprises against Muslims, such as the efforts of the Normans of southern Italy to reconquer Sicily. The description of the battle of Cerami in Sicily in 1063 by Gaufredus Malaterra implies that the expedition of which this was an incident was regarded as a Crusade. For the ordinary soldier this character of the expedition was confirmed by the appearance of Saint George. Still farther afield, when a naval expedition against Tunisia was organized jointly in 1087 by Pisa, Genoa, Rome and Amalfi, it was given a banner by the Pope.

Papal policy supported men in numerous efforts against enemies of Christendom, and not exclusively against Muslims. For the invasion of England in 1066 William the Conqueror had the papal blessing and a papal banner. A little earlier in 1059 the Pope had made a treaty with the Norman knights in southern Italy who were fighting the Byzantines, that is, against Orthodox Christians. Expeditions against the pagans of eastern Europe naturally had full papal approval. The conception of the Crusade was even used against heretics within Christendom, notably in 1209 against the Cathars or Albigensians in southern France.

The reforming Papacy from the middle of the eleventh century thus played a major part in shaping and defining the conception of Crusade. In this conception were fused together ideas about the functions of the Christian king, the Christian knight and the Christian pilgrim. There was a further advantage in the conception of the Crusade, however, namely, that it gave direction to many secular forces of the time, especially to the new energies which were bursting forth in northern France and the surrounding lands. Because of this it is difficult to determine in the case of a particular expedition or particular individual the precise balance of religious and secular interests. Sometimes there was deep religious fervour, but at other times worldly concerns predominated. One has the impression, for example, that the Reconquista in Spain had more religious feeling attached to it than had the Norman conquest of southern Italy and Sicily, at least so far as the leaders are considered.

The launching of the Crusades and their course[5]

Under the reforming Popes with their centralizing tendencies curial policy came to embrace not merely the whole of western Christendom, but also its relations to its Christian neighbours in the east. In 1054 relations became strained between Rome and Constantinople because of a quarrel between the Patriarch Michael Cerularius and Cardinal Humbert; but it is now realized that this was not, as was formerly thought, a complete schism between East and West. There was still communication between the two Christian centres, and some men on both sides worked for a reconciliation. Meanwhile the Byzantine empire suffered a great defeat by the Seljuq Turks at Manzikert in 1071, and continued to be hard pressed by them and by pagans in Europe. When about 1095 Urban II (1088–99) received from the Byzantine emperor a request for military help, he saw that to provide help might lead to an improvement in ecclesiastical relations. The appeal in his speech at Clermont in 1095 was primarily for military support for the eastern Christians, and he linked this with the ideas that had been gradually developing about fighting against the enemies of Christendom.

At this point popular feeling in western Europe took over and modified the conception of Crusade which papal policy had slowly been elaborating. There was a great upsurge of the spirit, and the idea of Crusade fired the imaginations. Though the speech at Clermont seems to have said nothing about Jerusalem, what attracted ordinary men more and more was the prospect of recovering Jerusalem and making the pilgrimage to the holy places in Palestine. Masses of men were deeply stirred, and in the enthusiasm of the moment often acted recklessly, like the followers of Peter the Hermit. The Crusading movement soon acquired a momentum of its own. Even when the religious idealism evaporated, political leaders still thought there were advantages in using the conception of Crusade. So powerful was the conception for a time that in western Europe, with a metaphorical interpretation, it still has some vestigial influence.

There was a phenomenal response to the appeal made at Clermont, and the Byzantine emperor was probably alarmed at the size of the western armies which converged on Constantinople in 1097. The way in which the Crusading idea had developed, however, made it necessary for these armies to push on southwards towards Jerusalem. The capture of the city in 1099 and the establishment of the kingdom of Jerusalem (with subordinate statelets at Edessa, Antioch and Tripoli) were felt to mark the achievement of the aims of the Crusading movement. This measure of success, however, was due to the disunity of the Muslims throughout the region, with several leaders struggling against one another. When the atabeg of Mosul overcame various rivals and increased his strength, he was able to recover Edessa (1144). Then Saladin came on the scene in 1169, united Egypt and Syria under his rule, and inflicted a number of defeats on the Christians, culminating in the recapture of Jerusalem in 1187. The Third Crusade (1189–92) was a response to this disaster. It recovered Acre in 1191 after a two-year siege but made no further progress, and the Crusaders had to be content with a narrow strip of territory along the coast. After this discouragement it is perhaps not surprising that secular interests were able to divert the Fourth Crusade to the capture of Constantinople itself in 1204.

Popular interest continued to be centred in Jerusalem, and quarrels among the successors of Saladin enabled the Franks to occupy it once again from 1229 to 1244, this time by treaty. About 1250 power in Egypt and Syria passed from the Ayyūbids (the dynasty of Saladin) to the Mamlūks, and the pressure these were soon able to exercise on the Crusaders led to a gradual reduction of the latter's territory. After the Mamlūks took Acre by storm in 1291, the remaining coastal towns fell within a month or two. The attempt to recover Jerusalem for the Christians had failed utterly.

Even after this final disaster a few men continued to dream of winning Jerusalem again for Christendom. After the reverses of the twelfth century western Europeans had a clearer realization of the great strength of the Islamic states as a whole. Leaders came to think in terms of a broader and more sophisticated strategy, and to appreciate the impossibility of maintaining their foothold in Palestine and Syria unless they controlled either Asia Minor or Egypt. Ideas of this kind lay behind the landing in Egypt in 1249 by King Louis of France and also his expedition to Tunisia in 1270. About 1313 a Dominican friar, Guillaume Adam, who had travelled in Persia, India and Ethiopia, wrote a book entitled *De modo Saracenos extirpandi*, and in this suggested among other things the commissioning of a Christian fleet in the Indian Ocean. Thoughts on the wider strategic problems of holding Jerusalem are also found in fourteenth-century writers on Crusading aims such as Ramon Lull, Marino Sanudo and Philippe de Mézières. Thus the conception of the Crusade persisted even when the actual holders of power were no longer prepared to take any active steps to realize it.

The significance of the Crusades for Europe

The student of Islam who turns to look at medieval Europe is struck above all by two things. One is the way in which a distorted image of Islam took shape in Europe between the twelfth and fourteenth centuries, and has to some extent continued to dominate European thinking ever since; this point will be considered more fully in the last lecture. The other matter is the extraordinary way in which the Crusading idea gripped the hearts and minds of western Europeans. It is all the more amazing when one considers how quixotic and foolhardy the whole series of enterprises was. There was no realization of the military strength of the lands of the Levant, and little of the physical conditions under which men would be fighting. How could the Crusading leaders, with the existing means of transport, have contemplated moving their armies over the enormous distances involved? Let us then look at various factors which may help to explain the vigour of the Crusading movement.

From what has already been said about the growth of the

idea of Crusade it is clear that in this idea as it developed after 1095 various strands of religious idealism were woven together. Certain secular tendencies and forces, however, also found a focus in the Crusading aim of recovering the holy places by military means. Many parts of western Europe had been experiencing greater material prosperity. Trade was flourishing and wealth increasing. There was a feeling of buoyancy and self-confidence. In some sections of society, however, life had become difficult. There were many younger sons of the nobility, for example, for whom the family estates could not now provide the standard of living which they had come to expect. For this reason and others much of the energy of the upper classes was spent in fighting one another. The Popes looked for a greater measure of harmony and peace in Catholic lands, and saw that this might be attained if military efforts were directed against the infidel. By the end of the eleventh century, too, the experiences of the Norman knights in southern Italy had shown that the knight in armour had great military potentialities, since a few resolute knights acting together could control vast regions, and in the process win new estates for themselves.

All this, however, does not explain why the Crusade should come to be directed chiefly to Jerusalem and against Muslims, and why more effort was not devoted, for example, to expansion into north-eastern Europe. On the religious side there was the idea of pilgrimage, and for Christians Jerusalem was the goal of pilgrimage *par excellence*. On the secular side the commercial ambitions of several Italian cities may have played a part. The paramount fact, however, was that for centuries Islam had been the great enemy, controlling the Mediterranean from Spain to Syria, and extending its sway eastwards and southwards apparently without limit. Even after 1100 western Europeans still thought that the Muslims occupied more than half the world. Many were also aware of the cultural superiority of the Arabs; and those who had met Arabs in Spain, Sicily or elsewhere had witnessed their serene and confident belief in the superiority of their religion. Some Christians may even have felt – in accordance with one aspect of Old Testament teaching – that the material prosperity of the Arabs was a sign of divine favour. In short, the attitude of western Europeans towards

Arab Muslims was essentially one which combined deep fear with no small degree of admiration.

By 1095 various events had occurred which made the western Europeans less fearful and more ready to challenge the Arabs militarily. The capture of Toledo in 1085 was an important step in the Spanish Reconquista, and the Norman conquest of Sicily had been completed in 1091. Men from northern France in particular had been active in several phases of the Reconquista. It was in northern France, too, about this time that the *Song of Roland* took shape, to be followed by other *chansons de geste*; and here we have an influential popular presentation of the ideal of the Frankish knight in which his chief enemies are the Saracens. Thus a number of factors, some material, some spiritual or psychological, combined to make men eager for warfare against the Saracens above all. Many found a satisfying identity for themselves in the conception of the Christian warrior; and they heightened the ideal character of this conception by directing the warfare against the enemy they had once feared most and whom they still saw to be superior in certain ways.

The fundamental significance of the Crusading movement, then, was that through this movement western Europe found its soul. This positive result far outweighed the political and military failure. Despite this failure Europe continued for other reasons to progress. Eastern Christendom, on the other hand, was seriously weakened by the Crusades, and eventually succumbed to the Ottoman Turks; in this respect the result of the Crusades was the exact opposite of their professed aim. Culturally the Crusaders in the East experienced some of the attractive sides of Islamic life, and attempted to imitate these on their return home. A few translations from Arabic into Latin were made in the Crusading states. On the whole, however, the spread of Arab material and intellectual culture in Europe came about chiefly through the Arab presence in Spain and Sicily.

Finally the idea of Crusade made a small contribution to the movement of exploration which led to the discovery of America and of the route to India round the Cape of Good Hope. As a result of Crusading expeditions and commercial operations eastwards western Europeans came to realize that beyond the Islamic states there were other states which were neither Islamic nor Christian. When the advance to Jerusalem through the Mediterranean or eastern Europe was proved to be impracticable, a few men began to wonder if the Saracens could be attacked in the rear. The suggestion of a Christian fleet in the Indian Ocean was doubtless never taken seriously, but it was probably not entirely forgotten, and so came to be one minor aspect of the quest for the Indies, whether round Africa or across the Atlantic. Certainly some of those who sponsored or participated in the exploring expeditions regarded these as a Crusading enterprise, and the members of the expeditions bore the Crusaders' cross.

The profound positive significance of the Crusades for western Europe is in strong contrast to their lack of deep significance for the Islamic world. Essentially they are no more for Muslims than a series of frontier incidents. There will be an opportunity in the last lecture to look more closely at the contrast.

FIVE

SCIENCE AND PHILOSOPHY IN EUROPE

In the last lecture it was emphasized that the attitude of western Europe to the Arabs contained two contrasting elements, deep fear on the one hand, and on the other admiration coupled with an acknowledgement of superiority. The fear was considerably allayed by the end of the eleventh century, with the capture of Toledo in 1085, the completion of the conquest of Sicily in 1091 and the fall of Jerusalem in 1099. Perhaps this allaying of the fear made it easier for western Europeans to devote attention to what they admired in the intellectual culture of the Arabs. Perhaps, even if there had been no military victories, they would have studied Arab science all the same. Certainly it was in the twelfth century that European scholars interested in science and philosophy came to appreciate how much they had to learn from the Arabs, and set about studying Arabic works in these disciplines and translating the chief of them into Latin.[1]

First contacts with Arab science

Prior to the great period of translation in the twelfth century there were sporadic attempts to make progress in the sciences. Some small pieces of evidence indicate that the work of translation into Latin began in the ninth century. The first scholar of importance, however, to study Arabic science was Gerbert of Aurillac, who became Pope as Sylvester II (999–1003). In the course of his ecclesiastical career Gerbert acquired a high reputation as a teacher, and was specially competent in logic and Latin literature. He was also interested in the sciences, however. While he was in his early twenties he spent three years in Catalonia (967–70) and studied mathematics under one of the bishops there, and probably also astronomy. There is a colourful later legend about how he visited Cordova, studied 'the forbidden sciences' under a Saracen teacher, seduced his daughter and stole his books. This is all to be rejected. There is nothing to suggest that he learned Arabic himself; but it is known that the Catalonian monastery of Ripoll had a relatively good library, which included translations from Arabic works on the sciences. In both mathematics and astronomy Gerbert was far ahead of any Christian scholar of the time. He was also very practical and supervised the construction of various models as 'teaching aids' for his exposition of the Ptolemaic conception of the universe. He was probably also familiar with the astrolabe. In the field of mathematics he constructed a new form of abacus; and this is the first recorded use of Arabic numerals in Europe, but it was not followed by their general acceptance. In these respects Gerbert was far ahead of his time.

There are some other pieces of information from the tenth and eleventh centuries. A tenth-century manuscript at Ripoll contains two Latin treatises on the astrolabe which must be from Arab sources. It is known that about 1025 there was an astrolabe at Liège; and two further books on the astrolabe (dated about 1048 and incorporating Arab teaching) have been attributed to a German scholar, Hermannus Contractus, though the attribution is doubtful. Such scraps of information, however, are sufficient to show that it was from Spain that a knowledge of mathematics and astronomy spread into Europe.

Knowledge of medicine, on the other hand, came by a different route, and is chiefly associated with the very old school of medicine at Salerno. In the tenth century a Jew, usually called Donnolo, who had been a prisoner of the Saracens wrote some medical treatises for the school in Hebrew; and these would contain elements of Arab medicine. The chief advance or 'break-through', however, was made about a century later by a man called 'Constantine the African'; his original name is unknown. According to the usual accounts, he gained a livelihood as a merchant travelling between Tunisia and southern Italy, perhaps dealing in drugs. On a visit to Salerno he realized how backward the school there was, and for reasons unknown to us decided to go and study medicine in the Islamic world. After a time he returned to Salerno. Much of this may be legendary, but it is certain that he spent the final part of his life at the Benedictine monastery of Monte Cassino, translating into Latin the medical works he had studied. Among these was the *Liber regius*, the compendium on medicine, of the tenth century Iraqi physician whom Europe came to know as Haly Abbas.

The great period of translation

Many manuscripts exist with translations of Arabic works into Latin, but it is now thought by the experts that frequently the ascription of a translation to a particular translator is no more than a later guess. There are also difficulties about the identity of some of the translators. Thus while the account of the translation movement is sound in general, it is subject to correction in detail.

After the Christian conquest of Toledo in 1085 many Muslims and Arabic-speaking Jews continued to live there. Raimundo, archbishop of Toledo from 1125 until his death in 1151, realized that this situation presented a great opportunity, and encouraged scholars to go to Toledo. He met Peter the Venerable when the latter visited Spain in 1142, and may have aided the translation project. The two most notable translators, however, are now known not to have been active in Toledo until after Raimundo's death. One of these, Dominic Gundisalvi (Domingo Gonzalez), archdeacon of Segovia, had as Arabic-speaking collaborators Avendeath (Ibn-Dā'ūd; a Jew who had become a Christian) and John of Seville (Johannes Hispalensis) – the two are almost certainly distinct and neither is to be identified with the later Juan Hispano. Probably Gundisalvi chose the work to be translated and gave the Latin text its final form, while the collaborator rendered the sense of the Arabic into Latin. Most twelfth-century translations seem to have been produced in this way by two scholars working together. The other great translator was Gerard of Cremona, an Italian who came to Toledo and worked there for many years until his death in 1187. To him are ascribed about a hundred translations. It has been suggested that he had a team of translators working under him, and he is known to have collaborated with a Mozarab Christian called Ghālib or Galippus. Another suggestion is that Gerard of Cremona is the name which later scholars attached to a translation when they were in doubt.

Other parts of Spain also contributed to the work of translation in the twelfth century. Rather earlier than Gundisalvi was Hugh of Santalla who translated scientific works for the bishop of Tarazona, a small town west of Saragossa. About the same time in the same region two scholars from beyond the Pyrenees were together translating works of astronomy and meteorology when they were diverted to some theological translations (to be mentioned in the next lecture) by the Abbot Peter the Venerable. The scholars were Hermann of Dalmatia and an Englishman, Robert of Ketton, who became archdeacon of Pamplona. On the eastern coast at Barcelona an Italian, Plato of Tivoli, in association with Abraham bar Ḥiyya, was translating works of geometry and astronomy from both Hebrew and Arabic.

From the Crusading states of the east came only one or two translations. The chief was that of the medical compendium of Haly Abbas made by Stephen of Pisa (or of Antioch). Syria was also visited by Adelard of Bath, an Englishman who had studied in France and spent some time in Sicily. It is probable that he also studied in Islamic Spain, though there is no actual record of this; he was certainly aware of recent developments in Arab scientific scholarship. He had been educated in the tradition of the cathedral schools, but he became one of the most influential pioneers of the scientific spirit. His translations include the astronomical tables of al-Khwārizmī and the *Elements* of Euclid.

By the thirteenth century there was a vigorous intellectual movement in western Europe, capable of assimilating all the Arabs had learned in science and philosophy and of moving on to fresh discoveries. The remaining Arabic works of merit were now translated, in so far as the Europeans were interested in them. The outstanding figure is Michael Scot, who died in or before 1236, probably in Scotland. Subsequently many legends grew up around his name. He was called a 'wizard' and credited with vast magical powers, thus gaining a place in Dante's *Inferno*. The allegation that he feasted his friends on dishes brought physically from the royal kitchens of France and Spain may be an exaggerated expression of the fact that rising gastronomical standards in Europe were due to Moorish cuisine. Michael is known to have been in Toledo in 1217, then in Bologna, then in Rome, from which he was commended by the Pope to the Archbishop of Canterbury. He found a more congenial environment, however, at the Sicilian court of Frederick II of Hohenstaufen, who was personally interested in the various branches of Arab science; and it was for him that some of Michael's translations were made. These included scientific and philosophical works by Aristotle, commentaries on these by Averroes, and a work of Avicenna on natural history.

Another important name from the thirteenth century is that of Alfonso X of Castile, the Wise (1252–84). Because of his keen personal interest he commissioned translations of scientific and historical works, and he was also the founder of several institutions of higher education.[2] Some of the translations were made into Latin, but others were into the Spanish of Castile, which had just been made the official language of the country. The close of the thirteenth century marked the end of the great age of translation from Arabic into Latin, though a few translations were still being made into Latin in the sixteenth and even seventeenth centuries. It was through the earlier translations, however, that Arab science and philosophy made its great impact on the intellectual life of western Europe. By the thirteenth century the Europeans themselves had attained a great measure of competence in science and philosophy.

Finally a word must be said about the Jewish share in the transmission of Arab science and philosophy to Europe. As in other Islamic states the Jews in Spain were a 'protected minority' (*ahl adh-dhimma*); but they were on good terms with the Arabs, because they had helped them against the Visigoths at the conquest, and because the Arabs themselves were a minority in Spain. In the middle of the tenth century we find that Ḥasdāi ibn-Shaprūṭ had become court physician to ʿAbd-ar-Raḥmān III, had proved a successful diplomat in the service of the caliph, and had also established in Spain a group of Talmudic scholars. From the latter there developed the use of Hebrew as a learned language. For ordinary purposes the Jews had hitherto used either Arabic or the Romance dialect of the country. Some Jews studied science and philosophy with Arab scholars and became experts in these disciplines. Some wrote in Arabic, like Ibn-Gabirol or Avicebron (d. 1058) and Maimonides (d. 1204). In the early twelfth century translations began to be made into Hebrew of Arabic scientific works, and original works were also composed in Hebrew. One of the best known of these Jewish scholars was Ibn-Ezra or Abraham Judaeus (d. 1167). In the thirteenth and fourteenth centuries Jewish scholarship flourished not merely in Spain but also in southern France and elsewhere. In some cases Hebrew works were translated into Latin; but apart from this the Jews were important as transmitters of Arab science and philosophy since they were often in close touch with the Christian scholars of western Europe.

For the rest of this lecture I propose to look at the different disciplines and to indicate in respect of each how the work of the Arabs was first assimilated and then surpassed.

The development of mathematics and astronomy in Europe[3]

Gerbert of Aurillac does not appear to have had any immediate disciples in his mathematical studies, and the great advantages of Arabic numerals were not immediately recognized. In the field of astronomy a trickle of interest can be traced from early studies in Lorraine and elsewhere. In both cases, however, it was not until the twelfth century that the disciplines effectively took root in Europe.

It is convenient to begin by describing the adoption of Arabic numerals, though chronologically it belongs to the thirteenth century. Hitherto western Europe had used the clumsy Roman numerals, which greatly increased the difficulty of most mathematical operations and seriously retarded the study of mathematical theory. A few men here and there may have known of the Greek sexagesimal system. The effective introduction of Arabic numerals is generally held to have taken place through the publication in 1202 of the *Liber abaci* of Leonardo Fibonacci of Pisa. In this book the writer showed how the 'ten signs' made possible the simplification and extension of arithmetical operations. The story of how Leonardo came to write the book is significant. His father was for a time in charge of the Pisan trading colony at Bougie in Algeria, and in his contacts with Muslim traders must have realized the superiority of Arabic numerals. To prepare his son for entering the family business he sent him to an Arab teacher of mathematics in Bougie. Perhaps other fathers did the same, but Leonardo had a streak of mathematical genius and is justifiably given a position of primacy. There is even an arabizing tendency in the form in which he gives his name in the book. He is 'Leonardus filius Bonacci', where Bonaccius is possibly a nickname representing an Arabic name like Ḥasan or Ṣāliḥ.

Once the utility of Arabic numerals had been demonstrated it was not long before they were used for most practical purposes. Along with the numerals various words have come into European languages. French 'chiffre', German 'Ziffer' and English 'cipher', and likewise French and English 'zero', all come from the Arabic *ṣifr* meaning 'empty'. The Arabic word was applied to the sign used to show that a particular position (units, tens, hundreds, etc.) was empty. Since this sign stood for a sophisticated idea, its original invention was later than that of the other nine figures; and some users of the nine figures found the use of zero difficult – they were in the habit of leaving the position blank. Nevertheless, or perhaps for just this reason, the word for the zero-sign came in some European languages to be applied to all ten figures. There is another Arabic word *sifr* (spelt differently in Arabic) meaning 'book' or 'writing', which is sometimes said to have affected European usage; but on the whole this is unlikely.

Some interest in astronomy had been generated by discussion of the Christian calendar in the Carolingian period, and, as already mentioned, there are traces of this interest in the succeeding centuries. Fresh advances based on Arab astronomy may be said to begin with a Spanish Jew who in 1106 became a Christian and took the name of Pedro Alfonso. Little has survived of his own writings on this subject, but he had great influence on the next generation of astronomers, especially in France and England. He came to England about 1110 as physician to the king (Henry I), and imparted much of his knowledge to a monk called Walcher, who came from Lorraine and had been making astronomical observations for some years. Walcher and Adelard of Bath, who may also have come under the influence of Pedro Alfonso, helped to form a scientific tradition which reached its height in Robert Grosseteste (d. 1253), who was for a time chancellor of the University of

Oxford. These men were not merely interested in natural phenomena but were genuinely imbued with a scientific attitude which emphasized observation and experiment. Grosseteste further insisted on the underlying mathematical structure of the material universe. By the time of Robert Grosseteste there were available a few translations of Greek works made directly from Greek, but the chief stimulus to the development of science had come from personal contact with the living Arab tradition and from the Latin translations of Arabic works.

Medicine in Europe[4]

Medical practice in Europe, before Arab influence made itself felt, seems to have been at a low ebb. There is a well-known description of the crudities of European treatment by an Arab writer of the Crusading period, Usāma ibn-Munqidh. The writer's uncle, a Muslim prince, had sent a doctor to a Frankish neighbour at the latter's request. When the doctor returned after a surprisingly short period, he had a remarkable tale to tell. He had had to treat a knight and a woman. The knight had an abscess on the leg, to which the Arab doctor applied a poultice to bring it to a head; the abscess burst and began to drain satisfactorily. The woman suffered from what is called 'dryness', though the precise nature of this condition is not clear. The Arab ordered a strict regimen, including abundant fresh vegetables. At this point a Frankish doctor came on the scene. He asked the knight whether he preferred to live with one leg or die with two. The knight gave the obvious answer, and the doctor made him stretch out his leg on a block of wood while a strong man tried to cut off the affected part with a sharp axe. The first stroke failed to sever the limb. The second caused the marrow to flow out, and the man died almost at once.

The treatment of the woman was even worse. The Frankish doctor declared that a demon had possessed her, and that her hair must be cut off. This was done, and the woman went back to her diet of garlick and mustard. The 'dryness' increased and the doctor ascribed this to the fact that the demon had entered into her head. He then made a cross-shaped incision, pulled the skin apart until the skull was exposed, and rubbed in salt. The woman died at once. Thereupon the Arab asked the people whether they had any further need of him, got a negative answer and returned home.

This story, taken by itself, reminds one of accounts of African witch-doctors by nineteenth-century missionaries! It is not, however, Usāma's final verdict on European medicine. He also records the cure of a badly infected leg by a Frankish physician, and describes a remedy for scrofula given by a Frank, and adds that he himself had tried out this method of treatment and found it effective. Though there is thus a contrast between Usāma's favourable and unfavourable judgements, it will be found, when the precise points at issue are noted, that there is coherence in Usāma's picture of European medicine. In the first story there is implied criticism, first of the ignorance of the physiological causes of the pathological condition, and second, of the ignorance of adequate surgical techniques. On the other hand, Usāma praises the Franks for their knowledge of the medicinal properties of certain mineral and vegetable substances.

European sources tend to bear out this view of the strength and weakness of European medicine. The oldest medical school is usually held to be that of Salerno, though its early history is obscure. The climate of the region was suited for the convalescence of sick persons, and there is mention of a Benedictine 'hospital' towards the end of the seventh century; this was presumably a hostel providing lodging rather than an institution where treatment was given. Yet one also hears of a corporation of doctors, at first under the bishopric, but later as an essentially secular institution. It was for this institution that translations were made by Donnolo and Constantine the African. One of Donnolo's books was an account of over a hundred drugs, mostly derived from plants; and Constantine may originally have been a dealer in drugs. Thus it would appear that *materia medica* must have constituted at least a large part of the studies at Salerno in the eleventh century. Before 1100, however, the study of anatomy had been added, pigs at first being used for the purposes of dissection and later the bodies of executed criminals.

Another early medical school, possibly an offshoot from Salerno, was that of Montpellier. In 1137 we hear of a student of arts from Paris who went on to study medicine at Montpellier.

The town had a relatively large Arab and Jewish population, including Arabic-speaking Christians, and in the early thirteenth century was in close relations with the Arab schools of southern Spain. Because of this the contribution of Montpellier to the development of European medicine on Arab lines is probably more important than is generally realized.

It was only slowly that surgery became an acceptable subject of study in the medical schools. Originally the surgeons were men of low social standing, looked down on by the teachers in the medical schools. As late as 1163 there was an ecclesiastical decree forbidding instruction in surgery as part of the medical curriculum. A change in the attitude to surgery probably came about as a result of the great widening of medical studies when translations from Arabic became available, and of the Crusaders' practical experience of Saracen medicine. By 1252 it was possible for Bruno da Longoburgo in Padua to produce an important work called *Chirurgica Magna*.

Crusading experience probably also led to the establishing about 1200 of the first hospitals in the sense of institutions solely for the sick; but these still fell below Arab standards in such matters as having separate wards for infectious diseases. Physicians visited the patients in the hospitals, but the first recorded case of a hospital with a resident physician is at Strassburg in 1500. Another Arab practice – clinical instruction to students in a hospital – was not copied in Europe until about 1550.

The continued dependence of Europe on Arab medicine until the fifteenth and sixteenth centuries is shown by the lists of early printed books. The first book of all was a commentary by Ferrari da Grado, professor at Pavia, on the ninth part of the *Continens*, the great medical encyclopaedia of Rhazes. The *Canon* of Avicenna came out in 1473 and again in 1475, and had reached its third printing before the first work of Galen was printed; up to 1500 sixteen editions of the *Canon* had been published. As it continued in use until after 1650, it has been claimed that it is the most studied medical work in all history. The *Canon* was followed by other works translated from Arabic, including some by Rhazes, Averroes, Ḥunayn ibn-Is'ḥāq, Isaac the Jew and Haly Abbas. A statistician has argued that the numbers of references in the standard early European works show conclusively that Arab influence was much greater than Greek. In the works of Ferrari da Grado, for example, Avicenna is cited more than three thousand times, Rhazes and Galen a thousand times each, and Hippocrates only a hundred times. In short, European medicine in the fifteenth and sixteenth centuries was still little more than an extension of Arab medicine.

Logic and metaphysics[5]

The year 1100 is a convenient vantage-point from which to survey the state of philosophical learning in Europe. In 1100 Anselm was coming to the end of his career and Peter Abelard was just about to begin. Classical learning had been kept alive in monasteries and cathedral schools, but the chief interest had been in the literary aspect. From the tenth century there had been some study of a restricted number of the logical works of Aristotle as translated and commented on by Boethius. This led to the development of dialectic. Since the whole life of society was within the framework of Christian dogma, and since education was under ecclesiastical auspices, it was natural that dialectic should be applied to dogma. In effect Anselm is supplying a dialectical or rational defence of the content of faith, and the outcome of his work is to present the faith as a coherent rational system. Abelard, a generation later, is more sophisticated; he starts from the contradictions to which dialectic leads, but directs his criticisms not against dialectic itself but against its improper use or application. Neither man, however, made any attempt to link Christian doctrine with a general metaphysical view. Indeed in Catholic Christendom about 1100 there was no such thing as a general metaphysical view.

There are interesting similarities and differences in the process by which the Arabs adopted Greek philosophy and that by which the western Europeans adopted Arab philosophy. The primary interest of the Arabs was in medicine and astronomy, but these disciplines always remained near the periphery of the intellectual life of the caliphate. Philosophy came to the notice of the Arabs because of its association with these other disciplines, but it was then seen to be relevant to their main intellectual effort, which consisted in arguments which were overtly theological but had an important political reference. In Europe, on the other hand, the main theological arguments had little political reference and were mostly internal to the ecclesiastical institution. At the same time interest in the particular sciences was widespread and managed to penetrate some of the schools. This was made easier by the general acceptance of the conception of the seven liberal arts – a conception which went back to the sixth century. The seven arts were divided into the *trivium* and the *quadrivium*, the former consisting of grammar, rhetoric and logic, and the latter of arithmetic, astronomy, geometry and music. Most monasteries and cathedral schools concentrated on the *trivium*, for in western Europe knowledge of the *quadrivium* was exiguous. Even when, in the first half of the twelfth century the school of Chartres under a series of distinguished teachers developed a Platonic form of *quadrivium*, they made little use of Arab science. Only gradually did the early translations become known. The work of Adelard of Bath entitled *De eodem et de diverso* is still in part based on Plato's *Timaeus*, but his *Natural Questions* helped to spread knowledge of Arab science.

The first original European writing in metaphysics as in many aspects of science came from translators. In particular Dominic Gundisalvi wrote works, partly based on Arabic sources, entitled 'On the immortality of the soul' and 'On the division of philosophy'. In dealing with the conception of God as the unmoved Mover he brought theology into relation with physics, as had been done, for example in Avicenna's *Kitāb ash-Shifā'* (known in Latin as *Sufficientia*) and in the summary of Avicennian views (*Maqāṣid al-falāsifa*) produced by Algazel. This linking of theology with physics and metaphysics led eventually to a new type of theological writing in Latin which reached its height in the philosophy of Aquinas.

There was a strong Augustinian and Platonic strain in European thought which the Neoplatonic teaching of Avicenna and others further supported. Somewhat at variance with this was the European tendency to empiricism in the practical arts, and to this the experimental side of Arabic science appealed. Nevertheless, when a rational justification of scientific method was required by the intellectual climate of the time, the men who provided this, notably Robert Grosseteste and

Roger Bacon (*c.* 1214–92), were men from the Platonic tradition.

The logical teaching of Aristotle had long been known in Europe, at least in part, through the works of Boethius. In the twelfth century there appeared translations of part of the *Organon* made directly from Greek, and then others from Arabic. A much fuller understanding of Aristotelianism, however, came above all from the translations of the works of Averroes, especially his commentaries on Aristotle's metaphysics. The translations belong to the thirteenth century, but some knowledge of the thought of Averroes may have reached the Latin philosophers before his death in 1198. Certainly Aristotelianism was quickly taken up by members of the Dominican order such as Albertus Magnus (c. 1206–80) and Thomas Aquinas (1226–74). The latter in particular achieved a complete assimilation of Aristotle into a theologically acceptable system of thought.

The influence of Averroes on European thought cannot be properly understood if it is closely linked with the 'Latin Averroism' of Siger of Brabant (*c.* 1235–*c.* 1282) and others. Among other things Siger taught that the conclusions of reason in its philosophical use may be contrary to the truths of revelation; but both are to be accepted. This is the theory of 'double truth', though Siger himself would not have used that term. Averroes had certainly held something like this, but he had softened the opposition by supposing that Qur'ānic texts could be interpreted in such a way that any contradiction was removed; and Arabic has richer possibilities of interpretation than Latin. The Latin Averroists made no such attempt to reconcile reason and revelation, and their contemporaries felt – probably rightly – that their position, when logically followed out, would eventually lead to the destruction of religion.

This use of the name of Latin Averroists should not mislead us into thinking that it was chiefly through them that Arabic thought, and in particular that of Averroes, influenced Europe. This is far from being so. Arabic thought provided European thought with new materials, and brought within its purview a whole new world of metaphysics. All strands of European thought had to take cognizance of the translations from Arabic, nor merely the Averroists and their opponents, the party of

St Thomas Aquinas, but also conservative Platonists like Bonaventura and scientifically-minded Platonists like Robert Grosseteste and Roger Bacon. The whole range of subsequent European philosophy was deeply indebted to the Arabic writers; and Thomas Aquinas owed just as much to the Aristotelianism of Averroes as did Siger of Brabant.

SIX

ISLAM AND EUROPEAN SELF-AWARENESS

In the course of the previous lectures I have tried to show how the Islamic presence in Spain and Sicily and numerous trade contacts there and elsewhere led to a diffusion of Islamic techniques and products. What was thus diffused, however, was not felt by the Europeans to be something foreign which threatened their own identity. Even the shared culture of Islamic Spain was regarded by Mozarab Christians as belonging to themselves just as much as to the Muslims. I have also noted how increasing prosperity and vitality in western Europe in the eleventh century led to the emergence of the Crusading movement and how this came to be directed chiefly against the Saracens. It was doubtless because of this same vitality that in the twelfth century European intellectuals came to study Islamic science and philosophy. Now that these different aspects of the relationship of Islam and western Europe have been studied, is it possible to say anything about the total significance for Europe of the relationship?

Before attempting to deal with this question of significance there is one more aspect to be mentioned. I said earlier that when the Islamic historian looks at medieval Europe he is impressed above all by two things; the spiritual or religious depth of the Crusading movement; and the way in which a distorted image of Islam has dominated thinking in Europe from the twelfth century almost until the present day. It is now time to say something about this distorted image.

The distorted image of Islam[1]

It was apparently the Crusading movement which led to a growth of scholarly interest in Islam as a religion among Europeans. Something was known about Islam previously, of course, partly through Byzantine sources, and partly through the contacts between Christians and Muslims in Spain. Such knowledge as there was, however, was inextricably mingled with error. The Saracens were regarded as idolaters who worshipped Muḥammad; or else he was regarded as a magician or even as the devil himself – witness the English word Mahound, which is a corruption of his name. Sexual licence and promiscuity were held to be authorized by the Islamic religion.

Not surprisingly some of the first to show a real understanding of Islam were men already mentioned as translators. Pedro de Alfonso, the converted Jew, early in the twelfth century, devoted one of his *Dialogues* to polemic against Islam. This work is outstanding for the accuracy of its information about Islam, but it contributed little to the formation of the image. More important were the translations made by the two students of astronomy, Robert of Ketton and Hermann of Dalmatia, when commissioned by Peter the Venerable about 1142. On the basis of these translations, especially Robert's Latin version of the Qur'ān, Peter the Venerable himself produced a summary of Islamic teaching (*Summa totius haeresis Saracenorum*) and a refutation of it (*Liber contra sectam sive haeresim Saracenorum*). These two works, together with the translations produced for Peter the Venerable – known together as the Toledan Collection or the Cluniac corpus – were the first scholarly works about Islam in Latin (apart from the *Dialogue* just mentioned). The *Summa* in particular was free from the crude errors hitherto current in Europe, and thus marked a considerable advance. At the same time it did much to shape the new image of Islam. During the following two centuries many details were added to fill out the image; but the process was virtually complete by the time Ricoldo da Monte Croce (d. 1321) wrote his 'Disputation against the Saracens and the Qur'ān', also known as *Improbatio alchorani*.

The four chief points in which the medieval image of Islam differs from that of modern impartial scholarship are the following: (*a*) the Islamic religion is falsehood and a deliberate perversion of the truth; (*b*) it is a religion of violence and the sword; (*c*) it is a religion of self-indulgence; and (*d*) Muḥammad is the Antichrist. Something may be said briefly about each of these points.

(a) *Islam as falsehood and a deliberate perversion of the truth.* In medieval Europe people's views of nature, man and God were so dominated by Biblical conceptions that they could not conceive that there could be alternative ways of expressing these views. Consequently, whenever the teaching of Islam differed from that of Christianity, the former must be false. The general tone of European thought on this matter can be illustrated by a passage from St Thomas Aquinas (*Summa contra Gentiles*, book I, chapter 6), who was one of the most moderate as well as the most gifted thinkers of the thirteenth century. After speaking of how the Christian faith is confirmed and supported by many signs and evidences, he insists that there is no such basis for those who, like Muḥammad, become founders of what be calls 'sects'. Apart from the 'carnal' attractions of Islam he mentions the naivety of the evidences or arguments adduced by Muḥammad, his mingling of the truth with unhistorical stories and false doctrines, and the absence of miracles to confirm his claim to be a prophet. His first followers are described as 'men not learned in divine matters... but *bestiales*, living in deserts'; presumably the suggestion here is that they accepted any claim uncritically. They were so numerous, however, that Muḥammad could compel others by military force to become Muslims. Although he claimed that the Bible foretold him, examination shows that 'he corrupts all the evidences of the Old and New Testaments'.

While Aquinas and many other writers were content to say that Muḥammad mixed truth and falsehood, a few went further and alleged that 'wherever he said something true, he mixed in poison which corrupted it'. The true statements could then be seen as honey, only added to conceal the poison. As one man put it, 'Notice throughout the whole book that with marvellous cunning, when he is going to say something ungodly or recalls having said it, he soon puts in something about fasting or about prayer or about praising God'.

This aspect of the image of Islam implies a contrasting aspect in the image of Christendom. The Bible was seen as the pure and unadulterated expression of divine truth, possessing an absolute form valid for all times and places. Christian teaching was held to appeal rationally to mature, educated and cultured men, and to be supported by sound historical evidence.

(b) *Islam as a religion of violence and the sword.* As has already been mentioned incidentally Muḥammad was thought, even by scholars like Aquinas, to have spread his religion by military force. It was also supposed to be an ordinance of the religion of the Saracens 'to rob, to make prisoner and to kill the adversaries of God and their prophet, and to persecute and destroy them in every way' (Pedro de Alfonso). One over-eager apologist for Crusades, Humbert of Romans, went so far as to say, 'they are so zealous for their religion that wherever they hold power they mercilessly behead every man who preaches against their religion'.

In this respect the European image of Islam is far from the truth. As explained in the first lecture, the choice between Islam and the sword was not imposed on Jews, Christians, and members of other recognized religions, but was restricted to idol-worshippers and was little heard of outside Arabia. The military activities of the Muslims, of which the histories are full, led only to political expansion; conversion to Islam came about through preaching or social pressure.

Implicit in the image of Islam as a religion of violence is the contrasting image of Christianity as a religion of peace which spread by persuasion. It is strange that men engaged in Crusades should believe that their own religion was one of peace, while that of their opponents was one of violence. Some writers realized that the conception of a religion of peace was an ideal rather than an actuality, and argued that the failure of bad Christians to observe the ideal was no objection to Christianity. The paradox is presumably to be explained by noting that the purpose of Crusade was not the forcible conversion of the enemy but, as St Thomas Aquinas later stated, the prevention of the infidel from hindering the Christian faith. Perhaps this included the recovery of lands rightly Christian.

(c) *Islam as a religion of self-indulgence.* In medieval European eyes Islam was a religion of self-indulgence, especially in sexual matters. Plurality of wives had a prominent place in the image of Islam. It was often thought that, apart from the length of a man's purse, there was no restriction on the number of wives a man might have. Writers who should have known that no more than four were allowed speak of a limit of seven or ten. Verses from the Qur'ān were often mistranslated to bring in an objectionable sexual reference where none was intended. At least one writer found a verse in the Qur'ān which he said permitted fornication. Others seemed to take a delight in multiplying details about the sexual life of Muslims. Unnatural or bestial forms of intercourse between spouses were said to be encouraged and much practised. Even homosexuality was said to be allowed by the Qur'ān. For some the climax of Islamic sexual licence came in the Qur'ānic pictures of Paradise. Great prominence was given to the houris or dark-eyed maidens assigned there to the believers, and this was felt to be specially scandalous. The marital life of Muḥammad himself was much criticized, though the criticisms were often based on exaggerations or false allegations.

For some details in this medieval picture there is a basis in reality. A Muslim may have four wives and in addition slave concubines, and may divorce a wife without specifying any cause. Marriages and divorces, however, are carefully regulated legal proceedings, and do not happen casually. In respect of sexual relationships outside marriage some Muslim communities are puritanical, and a girl who has an illegitimate baby may be killed by a member of her family because she has dishonoured it. Adultery between two married persons is punishable by stoning (as in the Bible), but the infliction of the penalty is so hedged about with legal conditions that it is seldom carried out. In the Qur'ānic Paradise there are indeed houris or alternatively 'pure spouses', but the greatest delight there is often held to be the vision of God. Thus the medieval image of Islamic sexuality is in many ways a travesty.

To the European the Muslim was also self-indulgent in other ways. The 'gracious living' of Islamic Spain and Sicily must have appeared as self-indulgence to those unable to enjoy such luxuries. The Qur'ān was said to teach men to break their oaths when that suited their convenience, and to declare that a man would go to Paradise without having performed any good acts, provided he had repeated the *shahāda* (the confession of faith). It was also supposed that the belief in fate prevalent among Muslims was made an excuse for laziness and drift. In this respect also the image of Islam contains a mixture of truth and falsehood. Islam attacks monasticism, and, if celibacy occurs, does not specially honour it; but it approves of most other forms of asceticism. The fast of Ramaḍān is a great feat of endurance, and is still shared in by large sections of the population in predominantly Muslim countries.

This aspect of the image of Islam implied that Christendom was not self-indulgent. The Christian ideal was certainly one of lifelong monogamous marriage, and even within marriage, it was widely held, sexual intercourse was not altogether a good thing – the generative powers of men were for the procreation of children and not for pleasure. Some further implications of these points about sexuality will appear presently.

(d) *Muḥammad as Antichrist*. For some European students of Islam it was not sufficient to say that the Qur'ān contained much falsehood and that Muḥammad was not a prophet. Peter the Venerable took up the idea of some Greek theologians that Islam was a Christian heresy, and said that Islam was worse than this and that Muslims should be regarded as heathens. The core of Christian thinking on this point was that, since Muḥammad was not a prophet and yet had founded a religion, he had been positively encouraging evil; and so he must be either the tool or the agent of the Devil. In this way Islam is placed at exactly the opposite pole from Christianity.

The contrasting image of Europe[2]

These, then, are the four chief aspects of the distorted image of Islam which was formed in Europe between the twelfth and fourteenth centuries; and they have implicit in them aspects of a corresponding and contrasting image of Catholic Christendom. Since this was the way in which western Europeans thought of themselves, this latter implicit image might also be called an image of western Europe. Christianity, it was held, was wholly true and appealed to men rationally. It was a religion of peace, converting men by persuasion; and it was a religion of asceticism, mortifying all 'carnal' desires. This image may never have been made fully explicit, but it was present by implication in the image of Islam.

That it was possible to give a systematic and rational account of the Christian faith was amply demonstrated by the thinkers of the twelfth and thirteenth centuries, and notably by St Thomas Aquinas, though to the immediately succeeding age he may not have seemed to be so far above his contemporaries as he does to us. The intellectual structure elaborated by Aquinas came as the culmination of a process which had been going on for more than a century. During this period Arab science and philosophy had given Europe a new conception of the world. The science had stimulated pre-existing practical interests, and from these scientific studies there had sprung a wider cosmological and metaphysical outlook. Though theology is not based on cosmology, a man cannot for long tolerate a radical disharmony between his cosmology and his religious beliefs. The European theologians therefore set about harmonizing Christian doctrine with the new science. Aquinas like many others accepted what had been learnt from the Arabs, especially in its Aristotelian form. Taking advantage of the work of predecessors, he achieved a remarkably coherent system of thought in which science, philosophy and religious doctrine were all harmoniously comprised. The Christian claim to appeal to men rationally could certainly be justified.

It must also be emphasized that Aquinas was fully aware of the presence of Islam on the frontiers of Christendom and of the challenge it presented. In the second chapter of the *Summa contra Gentiles* he states that his aim is 'to make manifest the truth which the Catholic faith proclaims'; and he then goes on to remark that, while against Jews and heretics one may use arguments from the Old and New Testaments respectively, against Muslims and pagans one must have recourse to natural reason. Natural reason, however, he holds, cannot prove every Christian doctrine, though it is able to demonstrate, for example, that God exists and that he is one. On the other hand, in the case of those Christian doctrines which are beyond the province of natural reason, like the doctrine of the Trinity, it can be shown that the objections to them are not substantiated by reason. The aim of the *Contra Gentiles* is thus the apologetic one of defending the Christian faith against objections and criticisms, and of doing so on the basis of natural reason without presupposing that the opponents accept the Bible. In this way the form of the work is determined, or at least moulded, by the existence of Islam as a problem for western Europeans; and Christianity is presented as superior not merely to Islam as understood by ordinary Muslims but also to the beliefs of philosophers like Avicenna and Averroes.

It is significant that a dominant position was ascribed to Aristotle by Thomist philosophy and by much later European thought. Classical studies had never wholly died out in Europe, because Latin had continued to be the language of learning. A little Greek was known, chiefly through contacts with the Byzantines, and in the twelfth century a few translations of Plato, Aristotle and other writers were made directly from Greek. The main philosophical influence at this period, however, was Avicenna, and according to recent studies he may have been even more important than has hitherto been realized; perhaps this was because he was congenial to the platonizing strand in Christian thought. The thirteenth century brought an increase in the influence of Aristotle, chiefly fostered by the translations of the works of Averroes, several of which were commentaries on Aristotle. What I would like to suggest here is that the Europeans were attracted to Aristotle, not simply by the inherent qualities of his philosophy, but also by the fact that he belonged in a sense to their own European tradition. That is to say, the assignment to Aristotle of a central position in philosophy and science is partly to be understood as one aspect of the European assertion of distinction from Islam. The purely negative activity of turning from Islam, especially when so much was being learnt from Arab science and philosophy, would have been difficult, if not impossible, without a positive complement. This positive complement was the appeal to Europe's classical (Greek and Roman) past.

Dante illustrates one stage of the process by which Europe distinguished itself from the Islamic world and identified itself with its classical heritage. Some of the main conceptions of the *Divine Comedy* probably came from Islamic sources; and Dante was aware of Europe's debt to Arabic philosophical writers. Yet what is noteworthy in his great work is the relative neglect of Islam. The distinction from Islam is marked by the presence of Muḥammad in Hell among the sowers of discord; yet far less is said about him than about the classical hero Ulysses. The contribution of Arabic philosophers is acknowledged by placing Avicenna and Averroes in Limbo; but they are only two in number, while there are a dozen Greeks and Romans, and in the 'philosophical family' Aristotle is 'the master of those who know'. On the positive side the whole work is full of classical references, and it is Virgil who is Dante's guide.

A further stage of the process can be observed as the Renaissance gets under way. Now the former admiration for things Arabic is replaced by revulsion. The Italian scholar, Pico della Mirandola (1463–94), who himself was well versed in Arabic, Aramaic and Hebrew, says at the beginning of one of his works, 'Leave to us in Heaven's name Pythagoras, Plato and Aristotle, and keep your Omar, your Alchabitius, your Abenzoar, your Abenragel'. In the thirteenth and fourteenth centuries there had been provision for a professor of Arabic at Salamanca (as well as at Bologna, Oxford, Paris and Rome); but in 1532, when a scholar from the Low Countries asked in Salamanca about instruction in Arabic, a distinguished Spaniard said to him, 'What concern have you with this barbaric language, Arabic? It is sufficient to know Latin and Greek. In my youth I was as foolish as you and took up Hebrew and Arabic; but I have long since given up these two last and devote myself entirely to Greek. Let me advise you to do the same.'

The different situation in the Islamic world

From this account of the distorted image of Islam which developed in Europe and the contrasting image of Christendom with its new intellectual basis, let us turn to look at the very different situation in the Islamic world. As I said before, when the Islamic historian looks at medieval European history, he is impressed above all by the vigour and depth of the Crusading movement and by the important place in the European outlook taken by the new image of Islam. The reason for his being so impressed is that there is nothing corresponding to these in the Islamic world.

When one thinks of the Crusades as a series of wars between western Christendom and the Islamic world, it is natural to expect that they have a comparable place in European and Islamic history; but this is far from being so. The lands to the east of the Mediterranean actually affected by the Crusaders were at the time of the fighting divided among a number of minor leaders, whose chief aims were to maintain their own personal position and to get the better of their local rivals. There was no motive for uniting them against the Franks, and on occasion some made alliances with Franks against other Muslims. It was this disunity of the Muslims that made possible the measure of success attained by the Crusaders. The main Islamic power at the time of the fall of Jerusalem was the Seljuq sultanate, which controlled Baghdad and most of the great eastern centres of Islamic culture, but had its effective capital at Ispahan, some six weeks' journey from the scene of the fighting. Men in Ispahan were certainly not worried about the invasion of a relatively small territory so far away. One sees how little the Crusades seem to have mattered to the great historian Ibn-Khaldūn (d. 1406). In his lengthy *Muqaddima* or *Introduction to History* the only references to the Crusades are in a few paragraphs about naval control of the Mediterranean and two or three sentences about the mosques and sacred buildings of Jerusalem.[3] In short the Crusades had no more importance for the greater part of the Islamic world than the wars on the North-west Frontier of India had for the British in the nineteenth century, and probably made less impression on the general public consciousness.

Failure to realize this difference of significance of the Crusades for Europe and for the Islamic world has led even distinguished historians of Europe to make exaggerated estimates of the effects of the Crusades on Islamic affairs. It has been claimed, for example, that they increased the disintegration of the ʿAbbāsid caliphate and distracted the Muslims from dealing adequately with the Mongol invasions. There is little foundation for such claims. The ʿAbbāsids had had virtually no political power since 945; if anything they were stronger after 1191 when Saladin, who as a Sunnite acknowledged them, had accomplished the downfall of the Fāṭimid dynasty of Cairo. As for resistance to the Mongols, this was primarily the responsibility of the eastern Islamic rulers who were unaffected by the Crusades. European historians also speak of the Crusades as altering Muslim attitudes to Christians; but it is doubtful if this happened except temporarily and locally among those in contact with the Crusaders. Some of the Muslim leaders declared they were fighting in a Jihād or Holy War, and the idea doubtless increased the enthusiasm of many of their men; but the conception of the Jihād was centuries old and had no repercussions in society in general. Muslims formed no new image of Christianity as a result of the Crusades; in a sense Muslims had had from the time of Muḥammad a distorted image of Christianity which sufficiently supported their belief in their own superiority.

The significance for Europe of the meeting with Islam

In the course of these lectures so far a vast tract of history has been briefly surveyed, and it now remains to make some assessment of the significance for western Christendom of its meeting with Islam.

The feeling of inferiority with which western Europe confronted Islamic civilization had various facets. Islamic technology was superior to European at many points and more luxuries were available to wealthy Muslims; but this was probably a minor factor. Militarily the Saracens had been feared in the past, but now the Norman knights were proving a match for them. The extent of Islamic rule, however, was formidable. In the early twelfth century men regarded the world as consisting of three parts, Asia, Africa and Europe. The largest of these, Asia, was thought to be almost entirely Muslim, and so was much of Africa, while not the whole of Europe was Christian. In this way it was supposed that nearly two-thirds of the world was Muslim. For any Christian who had come in contact with Muslims, too, their unshakable sense of superiority must have been disturbing. In general the feelings of western Europeans over against Islam were not unlike those of an underprivileged class in a great state. Like the underprivileged class they turned to religion in their effort to assert themselves against the privileged group, and in particular to what might be called two new forms of Christian belief, namely the cult of Saint James of Compostela and the Crusading movement. The pilgrimage to Compostela and the enthusiasm for the Crusade to Jerusalem were the twin foci of a popular religious movement.

The distortion of the image of Islam among Europeans was necessary to compensate them for this sense of inferiority.

One of the chief contributions to the new image was that of Peter the Venerable, both by commissioning the Toledan Collection and by himself composing the Summary of Islamic doctrine and the Refutation of it. This was shortly before the middle of the twelfth century, at a date when the assimilation of Arab science and philosophy had not proceeded very far. Thus European intellectual dependence on Islam had probably little to do with the sense of inferiority, though it is worth remembering that two of Peter's translators, Hermann of Dalmatia and Robert of Ketton, had been studying astronomy before he induced them to accept his commission. It follows that Peter the Venerable must have had some awareness of the new learning being taken over from the Saracens and may unconsciously have had a sense of inferiority with regard to it. The image of Islam created at this time by the Christian scholars enabled other Christians to feel that, when they fought against Muslims, they were fighting for light against darkness. The Muslims might be strong, but the Christians were now convinced that in religion they were superior.

The war of light and darkness sounds well, but in this post-Freudian world men realize that the darkness ascribed to one's enemies is a projection of the darkness in oneself that is not fully admitted. In this way the distorted image of Islam is to be regarded as a projection of the shadow-side of European man. The violence and the excessive sexuality ascribed to Saracens existed also in Europe, even if contrary to the Christian ideal. According to Christian theory sexuality was 'carnal', and what was 'carnal' prevented the soul, the true man, from attaining eternal life. It followed that monastic celibacy was a higher life than that of marriage. Yet one wonders whether ordinary men, even when they paid lip-service to the belief in the superiority of celibacy, did not in practice proceed on the assumption that the exercise of sexuality was a great good.

It is evidence of the growing self-awareness of European Christendom that some leading figures came to understand how 'Islam' in the image stood for what was evil in Europe itself. Of John Wycliffe, for example, who was active in the second half of the fourteenth century, a modern scholar has written:

> For him the main characteristics of Islam were also the main characteristics of the Western Church of his own day. This does not mean that he was favourably disposed towards Islam. On the contrary. The leading characteristics of both Islam and the Western Church, as he saw them, were pride, cupidity, the desire for power, the lust for possession, the gospel of violence, and the preference of human ingenuity to the word of God. These features in the West were the main cause both of the divisions within Christendom and of the division of the West from its neighbours.[4]

In speaking of the Western Church as a whole Wycliffe even uses the phrase 'we western Mahomets'. Because the distorted image had thus a deep meaning for the life of Europe itself, it is not surprising that it persisted for centuries.

When one keeps hold of all the facets of the medieval confrontation of Christianity and Islam, it is clear that the influence of Islam on western Christendom is greater than is usually realized. Not merely did Islam share with western Europe many material products and technological discoveries; not merely did it stimulate Europe intellectually in the fields of science and philosophy; but it provoked Europe into forming a new image of itself. Because Europe was reacting against Islam it belittled the influence of the Saracens and exaggerated its dependence on its Greek and Roman heritage. So today an important task for us western Europeans, as we move into the era of the one world, is to correct this false emphasis and to acknowledge fully our debt to the Arab and Islamic world.

APPENDIX

List of English words derived from Arabic

The following list contains English words which have passed through Arabic at some stage in their history. Many have come into Arabic from other languages. Since the chief interest of the list is to indicate our debt to medieval Islam, recent importations by travellers in Arab countries have been excluded; e.g. wadi. The list makes no claim to completeness, and includes words whose derivation is disputed (usually indicated by a question-mark). Many sources have been used of which the most comprehensive is: Karl Lokotsch, *Etymologisches Wörterbuch der europäischen Wörter orientalischen Ursprungs* (Heidelberg, 1927). Abbreviations used: Ar., Arabic; Fr., French; Gk., Greek; It., Italian; Lat., Latin (including medieval Latin); Pers., Persian; Port., Portuguese; Sansk., Sanskrit; Sp., Spanish; Turk., Turkish.

ABYSSINIA – Ar. *ḥabashī* (Abyssinian)
ADMIRAL – Ar. *amīr ar-raḥl* (chief of transport fleet), or *amīr al-baḥr* (commander by sea)
ADOBE – Ar. *aṭ-ṭūb* (brick)
ALBATROSS – Port. *alcadroz* – Ar. *al-qādūs* (jug, bird is so shaped)
ALCAIDE, ALCALDE – Ar. *al-qā'id*
ALCANNA (plant yielding henna) – Ar. *al-ḥinnā'*
ALCHEMY – Ar. *al-kīmiyā'* – Egyptian, *kemi*
ALCOHOL – Ar. *al-kuḥl, al-kaḥūl* (powder)
ALCOVE – Sp. *alcoba* – Ar. *al-qubba* (dome)
ALEMBIC – Ar. *al-anbīq* – Gk. *ambix*
ALEPPIN (material) – Aleppo – Ar. *ḥalab*
ALFA, HALFA (grass) – Ar. *ḥalfa*

ALFALFA – Ar. *al-faṣfaṣa*
ALGEBRA – Ar. *al-jabr* (restoration)
ALGORITHM – Ar. al-Khwārizmī (proper name)
ALKALI – Ar. *al-qalī* (potash)
ALKANET (plant yielding dye) – Ar. *al-ḥinnā'* (henna)
ALMAGEST – Ar. *al-majisṭī* – Gk.
ALMANACH – Ar. *al-munākh* (tale, etc.)
ALPACA – Ar. *al-*, Sp. *paco*
AMALGAM – Ar. *al-malgham* – Gk. *malagma*
AMBER – Ar. *'anbar*
AMICE – Sp. *almucio* – Ar. *al-mustaq* – Pers.
AMULET – (?) Ar. *ḥamā'il* (things carried)
ANILIN – Ar. *an-nīla* (indigo) – Sansk. *nīlas*
ANTIMONY – Ar. *ithmīd* – Coptic *stim*
APRICOT – Sp. *albaricoque* – Ar. – Lat. *praecox*
ARAB (horse), ARABESQUE – Ar. *'arab* (Arabs)
ARRACK – Ar. *'araq* (lit. sweat)
ARSENAL – Ar. *dār aṣ-ṣinā'a*
ARTICHOKE – Sp. *alcarchofo* – Ar. *al-kharshūf*
ASSASSIN – Ar. *ḥashīshiyyīn, ḥashshāshīn* (sellers or users of hashīsh)
ATLAS (cloth) – Ar. *aṭlas* (smooth)
AUBERGINE – Sp. *alberengena* – Ar. *al-bādinjān* – Pers.
AVERAGE – Sp. *averia* – Ar. *'awwār* (loss)
AZIMUTH – Ar. *as-sumūt* (ways, directions)
AZOTH (mercury) – Ar. *az-zāwūq*
AZURE – Ar. *lāzwardī* – Pers.; or Ar. *azraq* (blue)
BABOON – Ar. *maymūn* (lucky; ape)
BALCONY – Pers. *bālākhānä* (high house) – Ar. *bālā*
BALDACHINO – Ital. *baldacco* – Ar. *Baghdād*
BANANA – Ar. *banāna* (finger)
BARBERRY – Ar. *barbāris*
BARBICAN – Sp. *barbacana* – Pers. *bālākhānä* – Ar. *bālā*
BAROQUE – Port. *barroca* – Ar. *burqa* (uneven sand, etc.)
BARQUE, BARQUENTINE, BRIGANTINE – Sp. *barca* – Ar. *barsha*, (*bārija*) – Egyptian, *vā-rā* (ship of sun)
BEDOUIN – Ar. *badawiyyīn*
BENZINE, etc. – Ar. *lubān jāwī* (Javanese incense)
BERBERINE – Ar. *barbāris*
BERGAMOT – Ar. – Turk. *begarmudy* (royal pear)

BEZOAR – Sp. *bezoar* – Ar. – Pers. *pādzähr*
BISMUTH – Sp. *bismuto* – (?) Ar. *ithmīd* (antimony q.v.)
BLOUSE – Lat. *pelusia* – Ar. *balusī* – Egyptian *Pelusium*
BOMBASINE – Lat. *bombacium* – Ar. – Pers. *pänbä* (cotton) (Turk. *pembe*)
BORAX – Port. *borax* – Ar. *būraq* – Pers. *būräh*
BORAGE – Fr. *bourrache* – Ar. *abū-rāj* (father of sweat)
BUCKRAM, BARCHANT – Ar. *barrakān* (heavy material)
CABAS (work basket) – Ar. *qafas*
CABAYA – Ar. *qabā'* – Pers.
CABLE – Ar. *ḥabl* (rope)
CADI, CAUZEE – Ar. *qāḍī* (judge)
CALIBRE – Ar. *qālib* (model)
CALIPH – Sp. *califa* – Ar. *khalīfa*
CAMEL – Lat. *camelus* – Ar. *jamal*
CAMELIA – Germ. (Josef) *Kamell* – Ar. *jamal*
CAMELOT (material) – Ar. *jamal*
CAMPHOR – Ar. *kāfūr* – Sansk. *karpūra*
CANDY – Ar. *qand*, *qandī* (thickened sugar-cane juice)
CAPER – Sp. *alcaparra* – Ar. *kabbār* – Gk. *kapparis*
CARAFE – Sp. *garrafa* – Ar. *gharrāfa*
CARAT – Port. *quirate* – Lat. *carratus* – Ar. *qirāṭ*
CARAWAY – Ar. *karawiyya* (or karawiyā')
CARMINE – Lat. *carmesinus* – Ar. *qirmazī*, *qirmiz* – Sansk. *kṛmija* (worm)
CAROB – Ar. *kharrūba* – ? Assyrian
CHECK – Ar. – Pers. *shāh* (king) (used as name of game)
CHECKMATE – Ar. *shāh māt* (the king is dead)
CHEMISTRY – (as 'alchemy')
CHEQUE – Ar. *ṣakk* (deed, written agreement) or as 'check'
CHESS – Pers. *shāh*
CHIFFON – Old Fr. *chiffe* – Ar. *shiff* (fine cloth)
CID – Ar. *sayyid*
CINNABAR – Lat. *cinnābaris* – Ar. *zinjafr* – Pers.
CIVET (CAT), ZIBET – Ar. *zabād*
COFFEE – Ar. *qahwa*
COFFLE (train of slaves) – Ar. *qāfila*
COTTON – Ar. *quṭun*
COFFER – Old Fr. – Ar. *quffa* – Gk. *kophinos*
COLCOTHAR – Ar. *qulqutār* – Gk. *khalkanthē*

CRAMOISY – Ar. *qirmazī – qirmiz*
CRIMSON (see 'carmine')
CUBEB – Ar. *kabāb*
CUMIN – Gk. *kuminos*, cognate with Ar. *kammūn* – ? Assyrian
CUPOLA – Ar. *qubba* (dome)
CYPHER – Ar. *ṣifr* (empty)
DAM, DAMBROD (draughtsman, draught-board) – Sp. *ajedrez de la dama, ajedrez atama* – Ar. *ash-shiṭranj at-tāmm* (complete chess)
DAMAN (rock-badger) – Ar. *daman isrā'īl*
DAMASCENE, DAMASK – L. *damascenus* – Ar. *Dimishk*
DAMSON – i.e. *damascene plum*
DATE – Lat. *dactylus* – Sp. *dātil* – Ar. *daqal* (inferior date)
DEMI-JOHN – Ital. *damigiana* – Ar. *damajān* – Pers.
DHOW – Ar. *dāwa*
DIVAN – Ar. *dīwān* – Pers.
DRAGOMAN – Ar. *tarjumān* (interpreter)
DRUG – Ar. *dūrawā* (?)
DRUSE – Ar. *Durūz*
DURRA – Ar. *durra*
ELEMI – Sp. *elemi* – Ar. (*al-lāmī*)
ELIXIR – Ar. *al-iksīr* – (?) Gk. *xēron*
FAKIR – Ar. *faqīr*
FANFARE – Ar. *farfara* (?) (cf. Fr. *fanfaron*)
FATA MORGANA – It. – Ar. *marjān* (coral)
FELUCCA – Port. *falúa* – Sp. *haloque* – Ar. *ḥarrāqa*; or Ar. *falaka* (be round), *fulk*, *fulūka*
FELLAH, FELLAHEEN – Ar. *fallāḥīn*
FONDACO (inn) – It. – Ar. *funduq* – Gk. *pandocheion*
FRET (of guitar) – Ar. *farīda*, *fard*
FRIEZE – Sp. *frisco* – Ar. *ifrīz* – (?) Gk. *Phrygios*
GABELLE – Lat. *caballa* (tax) – Ar. *qabāla*
GALA – It. – Ar. *khil'a* (robe of honour)
GALINGALE – Lat. *galanga* – Ar. *khalanjān*
GALLANT – Sp. *galante* (well dressed) – Ar. *khil'a*
GAMASH (leggings) – (?) Sp. *guadamaci* – Ar. *ghadāmasī* (kind of leather)
GAZE, GAUZE – Sp. *gasa* – Ar. *qazz* (silk) – Pers. (prob. not from Gaza)

GAZELLE – Ar. *ghazāl*
GAZETTE – It. *gazzetta* (coin) – Lat. *gaza* – Ar. *kanz* – Pers. *gänj* (treasure)
GHAZAL (poem) – Ar. *ghazal*
GIAOUR, GUEBRE – Turk. – Pers. *gäbr* – (?) Ar. *kāfir* (unbeliever), or *jawara* (deviants)
GIBRALTAR – Ar. *jabal Ṭāriq* (mountain of *Ṭāriq*)
GINGER – Lat. *gingiber, zingiber* – Ar. *zanjabīl* – Sansk.
GIRAFFE – Ar. *zurāfa*
GUITAR (CITHER, CITOLE, GITTERN, ZITHER) – Sp. *guitarra* – Ar. *qītār* – Gk. *kithara*
GYPSUM – Ar. *jibs* – Gk. *gypsos*
HAKEEM, HAKIM – Ar. *ḥakīm* (doctor), *ḥākim* (governor)
HASHISH – Ar. *ḥashīsh*
HALICHORE, HALALCOR – Pers. – Ar.
HAZARD – Sp. *azar* – (?) Ar. *az-zahr* (root)
HENNA – Ar. *ḥinnā'*
HOOKA – Ar. *ḥuqqa* (water-pipe)
HOWDAH – Ar. *hawdaj*
IRADE (Sultan's decree) – Turk. – Ar. *irāda* (will)
JAR – Ar. *jarra*
JASMINE – Ar. *yasmīn* – Pers.
JERBOA – Ar. *yarbū'*
JUMP, JUPE (jacket, bodice) – Ar. *jubba*
JUMPER – Ar. *jubba* (probably)
JULEP (drink) – Ar. *julāb* – Pers. *gul-āb*
KALIUM (potassium) – Ar. *qalī*
KAVASS, KAWASS (armed servant, courier) – Ar. *qawwās*
KERMES (insect giving dye) – Ar. *qirmiz*; cf. Carmine
KISMET – Turk. – Ar. *qisma(t)*
KOHL (eye-shadow) – Ar. *kuḥl*
LAC, LACQUER, crimson LAKE – ? Ar. – Pers. *lāk* or Turk. *lāqa* – Sansk.
LADANUM, (?LAUDANUM) – Lat. – Ar. *lādan*
LANDAU – Ar. *al-andūl* – Sansk.
lapis-LAZULI – Lat. *lazulum* – Ar. *lāzwardī* – Pers.
LILAC – Ar. – Pers. *līlak*
LEMON – Ar. *līmūn* – Pers.
LOOFAH – Ar. *lūfa* (1887)
LUTE – Ar. *al-'ūd*

MAGAZINE — Ar. *makhāzin* (sing. *makhzan*)
MAMELUKE, etc. – Ar. *mamlūk* (slave)
MANCUS (coin) – Ar. *manqūsh*
MARABOU (stork) – Ar. *murābiṭ*
MARABOUT (holy man) – Ar. *murābiṭ*, *marbūṭ* (?)
MARCASITE – Ar. *marqashītā* – Aramaic
MAROQUIN (made of Morocco leather): see Morocco
MARZIPAN, MARCHPANE – Ar. *mawthabān* (king established) – Pers. *marzubān*
MASK, MASQUE, MASQUERADE – Sp. *máscara* – Ar. *maskhara*
MAT, MATT – Ar. *māt* (is dead)
MATACHIN (sword-dancer in fancy dress) – (?) Ar. *mutawajjihīn* (assuming mask)
MATE (in chess) – Ar. *māt* (is dead)
MATTRESS – It., Sp. – Ar. *maṭraḥ* (where something is thrown)
MINARET – Ar. *manāra*, *mināra*
MOCHA – Ar. *Mukha* (town)
MOHAIR – Ar. *mukhayyar* (choice)
MOIRÉ (fabric) – Ar. *mukhayyar*
MONSOON – Port. *monção* – Ar. *mawsim* (season)
MOROCCO – Ar. *Marākush* (town)
MOSQUE – Old Fr. *mosquete* – Sp. *mezquita* – Ar. *masjid*
MULATTO – (?) Ar. *muwallad*
MUMMY – Ar. *mūmiya* – Pers. *mūm* (wax)
MUSCAT, MUSCADINE, MUSCATEL – Provençal, *muscat* (adj. of *musc*) – Ar. *musk*, or *Masqaṭ*
MUSK – Fr. *musc* – Ar. *musk* – Pers. *mushk*
MUSKET – Ar. *mustaq*
MUSLIN – Ar. *Mōṣul*, *Mawṣil* (town)
MYRRH – Ar. *murr*, *murra*
NABOB – Ar. *nuwwāb*, pl. of *nā'ib* (deputy)
NACRE (mother of pearl) – Old Fr. *nacaire* – Ar. *naqqāra*
NADIR – Sp. *nadir* – Ar. *naẓir* (opposite, sc. of zenith)
NAKER (kettledrum) – Ar. *naqqāra* – Pers.?
NATRON – Ar. *naṭrūn* – Gk. – Hebrew *nēther*
NITRE – Ar. *naṭrūn*, *niṭrūn* – Gk. *nitron* — Hebrew
NORIA (water wheel) – Sp. – Ar. *nā'ūra*
OGIVE – Lat. *augivus*, cf. It. *auge* – Ar. *'awj*

ORANGE – Ar. *nāranj* – Pers. *nārang*
OTTOMAN – Turk. – Ar. *'Uthmān* (proper name)
PERCIVAL (name) – Ar. *fāris al-fāl* (rider of good luck)
POPINJAY – Old Fr. *papagai* – Ar. *babbaghā* (?)
RACE – Sp. *raza* – Ar. *ra's* (head)
RACKET – Fr. *raquette* – Ar. *rāḥa* (palm of hand)
RAZZIA – Ar. (dialects) *ghaziyya*, *ghāziya*
REALGAR (red arsenic) – Ar. *rahj al-ghār* (dust of the cave)
REAM – Old Fr. *rayme* – Ar. *rizma*
REBEC – It. *ribeba*, *ribeca* – Ar. *rabāb*
RICE – Old Fr. *ris* – Ar. *ruzz*, *aruzz*
RISK – Sp. *arrisco*, *risco* – Ar. *rizq* (sustenance)
ROB (fruit juice with honey) – Ar. *rubb*
ROC (bird) – Ar. *rukh* – ? Malay
ROCKET – Ar. *rāḥa* (palm of hand) (as 'racket')
ROOK (chess) – Ar. *rukh*
SACCHARIN – Lat. *saccharum* – Ar. *sukkar*
SACRE, SAKER (falcon) – Ar. *ṣaqr*
SAFARI – Swahili – Ar. *safara* (to travel)
SAFFRON – Fr. *safran* – Ar. *za'farān* – ?
SALEP, SALOP – (orchid) – Ar. *tha'lab* (fox, *sc.* testicle of)
SAMBOOK – Ar. *sanbūq*
SANDALWOOD – Ar. *ṣandal* – Sansk.
SAPPHIRE – Ar. *ṣafīr* – Sansk.
SARACEN – Lat. – Ar. *sharqī* (eastern)
SATIN – It. *setino* – Ar. *zaytūnī* (adjective from Chinese port)
SENNA – Ar. *sanā*
SEPOY – Turk. *sipāhī* – Ar. – Pers. *sipāh* (army)
SHELLAC a form of 'lac' (q.v.)
SHERBET – Turk. *sherbet* – Ar. *sharba(t)* (drink)
SHRUB (a cordial) – Ar. *shurb* (drink)
S(H)UMACH (plant) – Ar. *summāq*
SIROCCO – It. *scirocco* – Ar. *sharq* (east)
SOFA – Fr. – Ar. *ṣuffa*
SORBET – Turk. *shorbet* – Ar. *sharba(t)*
SPAHI – Turk. *sipāhī* – Ar. – Pers.
SPINACH – Old Fr. *espinage* – Ar. *isbānakh* – Pers. *aspanākh*
SUGAR – Fr., etc. – Ar. *sukkar* – Sansk. *sharkarā*
SULTAN – Ar. *sulṭān* (authority)
SULTANA – Ar. (wife of a sultan)

SYRUP – Old Fr. *sirop* – Ar. *sharab*, *shurb* (drink)
TABBY (cloth) – Ar. *'Attābiyya* (part of Baghdad)
TABOR, TABORIN, TABRET (drum) – Ar. ? *tabl* – Pers. *tabūrāk*
TALC – Ar. *ṭalq* – ? Pers.
TALISMAN – Ar. *ṭilasm* – Gk. *telesma*
TAMARIND – Ar. *tamr-hindī* (Indian dates)
TAMARISK – Lat. *tamariscus* – Ar. *tamr*
TAMBOUR (drum, etc.), TAMBOURINE – Ar. – Pers. *tabūrāk*
TARE – Ar. *ṭarḥa* (thrown away wrapping)
TARIFF – It. *tariffa* –Ar. *ta'rīf* (notification)
TAROT (cards) – It. *tarocco* – ? Ar.
TARRAGON – Lat. *tarchon* – Ar. *ṭarkhūn* – Pers.
TASS, TASSIE – Fr. *tasse* – Ar. *ṭass*, *ṭassa* – Pers. *tasht* (basin)
TEAK – Port. *teca* – Ar. *sāj* and Tamil *tekku* – Sansk. *śāka*
TOQUE – Ital. *tocca* – Ar. *ṭāqiya* (under-cap)
TROUBADOUR – ? Ar. *ṭarrāb* (singer); *ṭaraba* (sing)
TURBITH, TURPETH – Ar. *turbadh*
TUTTY – Ar. *tūtiyā'* (zinc oxide)
VIZIER – Ar. *wazīr*
WAD – Fr. *ouate* – Ar. *bāṭin*
ZEDOARY – Ar. *zidwār*
ZENITH – Old Fr. *cenit* – Ar. *samt* (*ar-ra's*; path of the head)
ZERO – It. *zero*, *zefro* – Ar. *ṣifr* (empty)
ZIRCON – Ar. *azraq* (blue)
ZOUAVE – *zawāwa* (name of tribe)

NOTES

Abbreviations

n. 2/13, etc.: note 13 to chapter 2, etc.
*EI*²: *Encyclopaedia of Islam* (new edition); see n. 1/1.
GAL; *S*: *Geschichte der Arabischen Literatur*; Supplementband; see n. 3/1.

Chapter One

1. Among general reference works on Islam the most important for the subject of these lectures are *The Encyclopaedia of Islam*, *Abstracta Islamica*, and J.D. Pearson's *Index Islamicus*. The first edition of the *Encyclopaedia* (four volumes and supplement, Leiden, 1913–42) is still required for the latter part of the alphabet. The second edition (Leiden and London, 1960–) is about half complete at the time of writing, and is cited as *EI*². The rubrics of the *Encyclopaedia* (with a few exceptions) are the Arabic terms, and thus the treatment of Islamic Spain comes in the article '(al-) Andalus'. The *Abstracta Islamica* appear annually as a supplement to the *Revue des Études Islamiques* published in Paris. The first *série* accompanied the *Revue* for 1927. The *Abstracta* are a classified list of both books and articles on Islamic subjects, and in some cases have brief indications of the contents. References will be given to the new classification introduced in 1963. Pearson's *Index Islamicus*, 1906–55 (Cambridge, 1958) lists all the articles on Islamic subjects contained in a wide range of periodicals. It is being continued by supplements at five-yearly intervals. The same classification of articles is used in the original volume and in the supplements. A brief bibliography will be found in the last two sections of Jean Sauvaget's *Introduction à l'histoire de l'Orient musulman* (second edition, Paris, 1961), 221-37; cf. the English revision.

The general topic of the lectures is dealt with, at least in part, in a number of works. A dozen essays on various aspects of Islamic influence are contained in *The Legacy of Islam*, edited by

Sir Thomas Arnold and Alfred Guillaume (Oxford, 1931). A new and completely rewritten edition is now in preparation under the editorship of Edmund Bosworth. Two volumes entitled *L'occidente e l'Islam nell alto medioevo* (Spoleto, 1965) contain the papers and discussions at a congress held at Spoleto in 1964 under the auspices of the Centro Italiano di Studi sull' Alto Medioevo. Sigrid Hunke's book *Allahs Sonne über dem Abendland; unser arabisches Erbe* (Stuttgart, 1960) is popularly written and based on wide scholarship, as is shown by the large bibliography especially of German works, but the author's strong feelings on the subject lead her to give a somewhat biassed account at certain points. Sir Hamilton Gibb's lecture on 'The Influence of Islamic Culture on medieval Europe' (*Bulletin of John Rylands Library*, xxxviii [1955], 82-98) has some useful observations. Other works which may be consulted are: Christopher Dawson, *Religion and the Rise of Western Culture* (London, 1950); Samuel C. Chew, *The Crescent and the Rose: Islam and England during the Renaissance* (Oxford, 1937); Stanwood Cobb, *Islamic Contributions to Civilization* (Washington, 1963); A. Malvezzi, *L'islamismo e la cultura europea*, (Florence, 1956).

2. The standard account of the early history of Islamic Spain is to be found in the three volumes by Évariste Lévi-Provençal entitled *Histoire de l'Espagne musulmane* (Paris, 1950–3). This replaces Reinhardt Dozy's *Histoire des musulmans d'Espagne, 711–1110* (Leiden, 1861; English translation, *Spanish Islam*, London, 1913) and also Lévi-Provençal's own version of that work (Paris, 1932). Unfortunately Lévi-Provençal died before carrying his own work beyond 1031. There is no single work covering the later centuries in any detail, though several scholars are engaged in researches on certain aspects of the period. Lévi-Provençal deals with the eleventh century in his revision of Dozy, but would probably have altered the treatment considerably had he lived to write his own account. The Almohad period is covered in detail by Ambrosio Huici Miranda in his *Historia politica del imperio almohade* (Tetuan, 1956–7).

A brief survey of the whole is given in Watt and Cachia, *A History of Islamic Spain* (Edinburgh, 1965), where there are further bibliographical details. Reference may also be made to Part IV (pp. 493-601) of Philip Hitti's *History of the Arabs* (seventh edition, London, 1961). In *Islam d'Espagne, une rencontre de l'Orient et de l'Occident* (Paris, 1958) Henri Terrasse uses his specialist knowledge of art and architecture to give a valuable interpretation of the significance of Islamic Spain.

Lévi-Provençal's general reflections on Islamic Spain are to be found in three lectures, first delivered in Egypt in 1938 and published as a book with the title *La civilisation arabe en Espagne, vue générale* (new edition, Paris, 1948). See also: *Encyclopaedia of Islam*, art. '(al-) Andalus' and arts. on individuals, dynasties and towns; *Abstracta Islamica*, section IA,7 'L'Occident musulman jusqu' au xve siècle'; *Index Islamicus*, sections XXXV (history) and XXXVII,h (literature).

3. The basic work on Sicily is Michele Amari, *Storia dei musulmani di Sicilia* (revised by C. Nallino), Catania, 1933–8. A briefer treatment by Aziz Ahmad is forthcoming in the Islamic Surveys Series. There is no single work dealing with the Arab penetration of Europe other than Spain. In *Muhammad and the Conquests of Islam* Francesco Gabrieli devoted pp. 199-204 to France, Italy and Sicily, and gives a further bibliography. The most recent works are: J. Lacam, *Les Sarrazins dans le haut moyen-âge français* (Paris, 1965); G. Musca, *L'emirato di Bari* (Bari, 1964). Cf. also U. Rizzitano in Spoleto Congress report (see n. 1), vol. i, 93-114; and Hitti, *History of the Arabs*, 602-14.

4. General works on Arab expansion include, besides that of Gabrieli mentioned in the previous note: Bernard Lewis, *The Arabs in History* (London, 1950, etc.); Robert Mantran, *L'expansion musulmane (VIIe-XIe siècles)* (Paris, 1969), with a large bibliography; John Bagot Glubb, *The Empire of the Arabs, A.D. 680-860* (London, 1963).

5. The Jihād or 'holy war' is discussed in Watt, *Islam and the Integration of Society* (London, 1961), 61f., 65-7, and *Islamic Political Thought* (Edinburgh, 1968), 14-19. The ostensible religious motivation of Christian-Muslim conflicts in the twelfth and thirteenth centuries is studied by John L. LaMonte under the title of 'Crusade and Jihād' in *The Arab Heritage*, edited by Nabih Amin Faris (Princeton, 1946), 159-98. The article '*Dj*ihād' by E. Tyan in *EI*[2] is concerned mainly with juristic aspects.

6. This line of thought is developed by Christopher Dawson in a chapter on 'The Expansion of Moslem Culture' in *The Making of Europe* (London, 1946), 118-34. Relevant too are the first three chapters of G.E. von Grunebaum's *Islam: Essays in the Nature and Growth of a Cultural Tradition* (American Anthropological Association Memoir No. 81; Menasha, 1955). Cf. further Watt, *Islam and the Integration of Society*, esp. chapters 6 and 7.

7. Cf. Louis Massignon, 'Le "hadith al-ruqya" musulman, première

version arabe du Pater', *Revue de l'histoire des religions*, cxxxiii (1941), 57-62; reprinted in *Opera Minora*, ed. Y. Moubarac (Beirut, 1963), i. 92-6.

8. The expansion of thought and of intellectual interest may be traced in the earlier stages of Arabic literature; cf. Sir Hamilton Gibb's *Arabic Literature, an Introduction* (Oxford, 1963, second revised edition); J.M. Abd-el-Jalil's *Histoire de la littérature arabe* (Paris, 1943, etc.); and Régis Blachère's *Histoire de la littérature arabe des origines à la fin du XVe siècle* (Paris, 1952-66, 3 vols.).
9. A detailed account of these matters will be found in Lévi-Provençal, *Histoire*, i. 118-26 (Charlemagne's expedition of 778 and his relations with Cordova and Harun ar-Rashīd), 225-39 (Christian opposition in Cordova). For the latter cf. also: Edward P. Colbert, *The Martyrs of Cordoba* 850–859: *a Study of the Sources* (Washington, 1962); James Waltz, 'The Significance of the Voluntary Martyrs of Ninth-century Cordoba', *Muslim World*, ix (1970), 143-59, 226-36; both these have further references.
10. French interests in Spain are exhaustively treated by Marcelin Defourneaux in *Les Français en Espagne aux XIe et XIIe* siècles (Paris, 1949).

Chapter Two

1. The book by Sir Thomas Arnold, misleadingly called *The Preaching of Islam* (second revised edition, London, 1913, etc.), is not about sermons, but is, as the subtitle states, *A History of the Propagation of the Muslim Faith*, sc. by peaceful means, and contains a vast store of facts on this topic.
2. Important recent articles are those by Claude Cahen and R.S. Lopez in the Spoleto Congress report (i. 391-432, 433-60). Economic activity in Islamic Spain is described by Lévi-Provençal in *Histoire*, iii. 233-324 (chapter 12, 'L'essor économique').
3. Pirenne's essay on 'Le mouvement économique et social' in G. Glotz's *Histoire du moyen âge*, viii: *La civilisation occidentale au moyen âge* (Paris, 1933) is translated into English in his *Economic and Social History of Medieval Europe* (London, 1937). The early expositions of his thesis about the effect on Europe of Arab expansion are described in the Preface to the posthumous *Mahomet et Charlemagne* (Paris, 1937; English translation, London, 1939). The details of the controversy raised by this work are only marginally relevant to the present study. One of his chief critics was R.S. Lopez who joined with

I. W. Raymond in *Medieval Trade in the Mediterranean World* (New York, 1955).

4. For Fraxinetum cf. Lévi-Provençal, *Histoire*, ii. 154-60.
5. Arnold Toynbee has an interesting account of the improvements in shipbuilding in *A Study of History*, ix (London, 1954), 364-8, with further references. On points of detail various articles in the *Encyclopaedia Britannica* may be consulted.
6. For al-Idrīsī see Mieli, *La science arabe* (n. 3/1), 198f.; *GAL*, i. 628 (*S*, i. 876f.); *Legacy of Islam*, 89-91; *EI*², art. '(al-) Idrīsī' by G. Oman with an extensive bibliography. For Arab geography in general there is a long article 'Djughrāfiyā' by S. Maqbul Ahmad in *EI*²; cf. also Mieli, §§ 14, 22, 32, 44, 48.
7. These matters are dealt with in Lévi-Provençal, *Histoire*, iii. 260-98.
8. On Arab forms of irrigation cf. Américo Castro, *The Structure of Spanish History* (n. 2/13), 98f.
9. On Arab influence in building cf. Castro, op. cit., 97f.
10. For the influence of Ziryab cf. Lévi-Provençal, *Histoire*, i. 268-72.
11. For the influence of Arab music cf. the article by H. G. Farmer in *The Legacy of Islam*, 356-75, and his *History of Arabian Music to the XIIth Century* (London, 1929).
12. Cf. Castro, op. cit., 98f.
13. The second view is that of Américo Castro in *The Structure of Spanish History* (Princeton, 1954), which is a revision of his *España en su historia: cristianos, moros y judios* (Buenos Ayres, 1948). This seems to be a more balanced treatment of the complex questions involved and certainly does more justice to the Arab elements in Spanish culture. The alternative view, emphasizing the continuity in the life of Catholic Spain since Visigothic times, is presented in the writings of C. Sanchez Albornoz, especially his paper in the Spoleto Congress report, i. 149-308, 'El Islam de España y el Occidente.' This way of regarding Spain seems to be parallel to the emphasis in western Europe generally on continuity with the culture of the Roman empire and neglect of the Arab contributions (cf. pp. 49, 79f. above).

    Other views have also been held. After the publication in 1832 of Washington Irving's *Tales of the Alhambra*, the imagination of Europe seems to have been caught by the romantic aspect of Moorish Spain. In this spirit *The Moors in Spain* (London, 1888) by Stanley Lane-Poole, who admired the Arabs but disliked contemporary Spaniards, presents the thesis that Spain's greatness was due to the Moors and that the decadence began when she expelled them.

14. The passage is quoted in Arnold, *Preaching of Islam*, 137f., and Watt and Cachia, *Islamic Spain*, 56. The original is from *Indiculus Luminosus*, §35 in Migne's *Patrologia Latina*, vol. 115. Alvar was connected with the Christian opposition in Cordova (cf. n. 1/9).
15. An interesting example of fusion is given by the Spanish words *albaricoque*, which has become the English 'apricot', and *albérchigo*, peach. The Arabic article 'al-' and the letter 'b', which in Arabic replaces 'p', show that these have come into Spanish from an arabized dialect; but at an earlier stage the words were derived from Latin *praecox* and *persica*, since the one fruit was considered 'early ripe' and the other a 'Persian' apple.
16. Much has been written on the relation of Provençal and Arabic poetry. Sir Hamilton Gibb in *The Legacy of Islam*, 180-209, emphasizes the stimulation of European poetry in the direction of romanticism; cf. also Pierre Cachia in Watt and Cachia, *Islamic Spain*, 159-61, 189f.
17. Quoted from Dawson, *Religion and the Rise of Western Culture*, 183f.

Chapter Three

1. For translations of Greek works into Arabic, the basic material is to be found in Moritz Steinschneider, *Die arabischen Übersetzungen aus dem Griechischen*, Graz, 1960 (reprinted from three periodicals dated 1889 to 1896). Manuscripts are listed under the names of the translators in Carl Brockelmann, *Geschichte der arabischen Literatur*, i (second edition, Leiden, 1943), 219-29; Erster Supplementband (Leiden, 1937), 362-71. (This is referred to elsewhere as *GAL, S.*) The translations are briefly described by De Lacy O'Leary in *How Greek Science passed to the Arabs* (London, 1949), 155-75. Cf. Watt, *Islamic Philosophy and Theology* (Edinburgh, 1962), 41-4. There is a short treatment of the translations (pp. 68-76) in the important compendium of Aldo Mieli, *La science arabe et son rôle dans l'évolution scientifique mondiale* (1938; reprinted 1966 with additional bibliography by A. Mazahéri); this is a valuable guide to the scientific thought of the Arabs with extensive references. Special attention is paid to Arabic science by George Sarton in his *Introduction to the History of Science* (Baltimore, 1927–48; esp. vols. i, ii and iii/1). Arab science is dealt with in *Abstracta Islamica*, section IIH, and in Pearson's *Index Islamicus*, section IV, b, c. In *EI*[2] see esp. 'Ḥunayn b. Isḥāk' (G. Strohmaier).
2. For mathematics and astronomy cf. *GAL*, i. 238-57, 617-26 (*S*, i. 381-402, 851-70); Mieli, *La science arabe*, §§15, 20, 21, 29,

37,43,48. The article in *The Legacy of Islam* (cf. n. 1/1) is by Carra de Vaux. Among relevant articles in *EI*² (n. 1/1) are: Baṭlāmiyūs (sc. Ptolemy; M. Plessner); (al-) Battānī (C.A. Nallino); (al-) Biṭrūdjī (J. Vernet); Djābir b. Aflaḥ (H. Suter); (al-) Farghānī (Suter, Vernet); Ibn Abī 'l-Ridjāl (D. Pingree); Ibn al-Haytham (J. Vernet); 'Ilm al-Hay'a (astronomy; D. Pingree); 'Ilm al-Ḥisāb (arithmetic, etc.; A.I. Sabra).

3. For medicine cf. *GAL*, i. 265-77, 635-51 (*S*. i. 412-26, 884-901), etc.; Mieli, *La science arabe*, §§16, 19, 23, 33, 38, 45, 50. Max Meyerhof is the author of an article on 'Science and Medicine' in *The Legacy of Islam*, 311-55 (and it is from this that the quotation on p. 56 comes). Among articles in *EI*² are: 'Ali b. 'Abbās (C. Elgood); Djālīnūs (Galen; R. Walzer); Ibn Sīnā (Avicenna; A.M. Goichon). A good general account was given by E. G. Browne in lectures published as *Arabian Medicine* (Cambridge, 1921; French tr. by H. P. J. Renaud, Paris, 1933). The present state of knowledge on the subject has been exhaustively treated by Manfred Ullman in *Die Medizin im Islam* (Leiden, *Handbuch der Orientalistik*, Ergänzungsband vi/1, 1970).

4. For chemistry and other sciences cf. *GAL*, i. 278-82, 651f. (S. i. 426-34, 902-4); Mieli, *La science arabe*, §§25, 31, etc.; and Meyerhof as in n. 3/3. Among articles in *EI*² are: (al-) Dīnawarī (B. Lewin); Djābir b. Ḥayyān (P. Kraus/M. Plessner); Ibn al-Bayṭār (J. Vernet).

5. For philosophy there is relatively a plethora of material. Cf. *GAL*, i. 229-38, 589-617 (*S*, i. 371-81, 812-51); etc. A useful bibliography (up to the date of publication) is *Arabische Philosophie* by P. J. De Menasce (Bibliographische Einführungen in das Studium der Philosophie, 6; Berne, 1948). Pearson's *Index Islamicus*, sections IV, a, b. *Abstracta Islamica*, IIG.

Christian philosophers writing in Arabic are treated by Georg Graf in *Geschichte der christlichen arabischen Literatur*, ii (Rome, 1947), 30-2, 109-18, 121-32, 153-6, 160f., 228f., 233-9, 252f., etc.

The best available general account of Islamic philosophy was for long that of Tjitje de Boer, *Geschichte der Philosophie im Islam* (Stuttgart, 1901; English tr. by E.R. Jones, London, 1903), but it is now somewhat dated. That of Goffredo Quadri, *La filosofia degli Arabi nel suo fiore* (Florence, two vols., 1939; French tr. by Roland Huret, Paris, one vol., 1947) tends to exaggerate the importance of Averroes. More balanced and better informed is the writing of Richard Walzer, most recently in his lectures at the Collège de France on, 'L'éveil de la philosophie islamique', *Revue des études islamiques*, xxxviii (1970), 7-42, 207-42; this deals specially with the translations, al-Kindī and al-Fārābī. *Greek into Arabic* (Oxford, 1962) by the same author is a collection of articles of which the first (pp. 1-28) is a brief sketch of Islamic philosophy down to Averroes. The first volume of Henri Corbin's *Histoire de la philosophie islamique* (Paris, 1964), which reaches Averroes, deals also with theology and science, and so devotes less space than might be expected to philosophy in the narrower sense; a special feature is the greater emphasis on Shīʿism and on thinkers from the eastern half of the Islamic world, and this should give a distinctive character to the second volume, when it appears. Cf. also Watt, *Islamic Philosophy and Theology* (n.3/1); the article on 'Philosophy and Theology' by Alfred Guillaume in *The Legacy of Islam* (239-83); and the following articles in *EI*²: Abū Ḥayyān al-Tawḥīdī (S.M. Stern); Akhlāḳ (sc. Ethics; R. Walzer); Falāsifa (Philosophers; R. Arnaldez); (al-) Fārābī (R. Walzer); Ibn Badjdja (sc. Avempace; D.M. Dunlop); Ibn Rushd (sc. Averroes; R. Arnaldez); Ibn Sīnā (sc. Avicenna; A.M. Goichon); Ibn Tufayl (sc. Abubacer; Carra de Vaux). Ikhwān al-Safā' (Y. Marquet). Several of the chief works of the Islamic philosophers have been translated into European languages.

Of those who approached philosophy from a theological standpoint the most important is al-Ghazālī or Algazel. His life and achievements, including his 'encounter with philosophy', are described in W. Montgomery Watt, *Muslim Intellectual* (Edinburgh, 1963). Many of his works are translated. His critique of the philosophers appeared as *The Incoherence of the Philosophers* (tr. by S.A.Kamali, Lahore, 1958); much of it will also be found in the refutation of it, translated by S. van den Bergh as *Averroes' Tahafut al-Tahafut* (*The Incoherence of the Incoherence*) in the Gibb Memorial Series (London, two vols., 1954). He gives a summary of his critique of philosophy in his autobiographical essay 'Deliverance from Error', which is translated in Watt, *The Faith and Practice of al-Ghazālī* (London, 1951), 19-85.

Much light is thrown on the use of Greek scientific and philosophical concepts by Islamic theologians by Josef van Ess in an article on 'Ḍirār b. ʿAmr und die "Cahmīya"; Biographie einer vergessenen Schule', *Der Islam*, xliii (1967), 241-79; xliv (1968), 1-70, 318-20. Cf. also S. Pines, *Beiträge zur islamischen Atomenlehre*, Berlin, 1936. The lack of enthusiasm among Muslims for science as such is illustrated by Gustav E. von Grunebaum in 'Muslim World View and Muslim science', in *Islam*,

Essays in the Nature and Growth of a Cultural Tradition (American Anthropological Association Memoir, No. 81; Menasha 1955), 111-26.

Chapter Four

1. For bibliography see n. 1/2.
2. In Santiago of Compostela there were fused Saint James the Greater (son of Zebedee) and Saint James the Less (or the Just, brother of the Lord), and there was often emphasis on the parallels between Santiago and the Lord. Because of the belief in the divine twins, Santiago was popularly regarded as *twin* brother of the Lord, though this view was unacceptable to orthodoxy; cf. Américo Castro, op. cit. (n. 2/13), 130-49. Castro thinks the Christian religious movement arose as a reaction to religious motivation among the Arabs, but there is little evidence for this, and it is more likely that the cult of Santiago was a response to the *political* domination of the Arabs, coupled with their self-confidence in matters of religion.
3. This section is based mainly on Carl Erdmann's fundamental work, *Die Entstehung des Kreuzzugsgedanken*, Stuttgart, 1935, 1955. He speaks of Brun of Querfurt on pp. 65, 97. Also relevant is *La chrétienté et l'idée de croisade* by P. Alphandéry (2 vols., Paris, 1954). The statement of Agobard about the meaning of the ruler's sword is quoted by Walter Ullmann in *A History of Political Thought: The Middle Ages* (Harmondsworth, 1965), 76. Maurice Keen in *The Pelican History of Medieval Europe* (Harmondsworth, 1969), 121, quotes a prayer for the blessing of a knight's sword.
4. Apart from general works dealing with the period, there is an important article by Gerd Tellenbach, 'Die Bedeutung des Reformpapsttums für die Einigung des Abendlandes', in *Studi Gregoriani*, ii, ed. G.B. Borino (Rome, 1947), 125-49.
5. For the Crusades reliance has been placed mainly on Sir Steven Runciman's *History of the Crusades* (Cambridge, 1951-4, 3 vols.; Harmondsworth, 1965). In *The Eastern Schism* (Oxford, 1955, etc.), he deals with the relations of the Papacy to the Eastern Churches in the 11th and 12th centuries. The crusades after 1291 are dealt with by Aziz S. Atiya in *The Crusade in the Later Middle Ages* (London, 1938). In *Criticism of the Crusade: a Study of Public Opinion and Crusade Propaganda* (Amsterdam, 1940) Palmer A. Throop looks at the failure of Gregory X (1271–6) to unite western Europe in the effort to hold the Holy Land.

   The question whether the Islamic idea of the Jihād influenced Christian conceptions is examined by Albrecht Noth in *Heiliger*

Krieg und Heiliger Kampf in Islam und Christentum (Bonn, 1966), and a mainly negative answer is given. In the article entitled 'Crusade and Jihād' (cf. n. 1/5) John L. LaMonte concludes 'in the twelfth and thirteenth centuries . . . religion played the same rôle that political ideology does today; neither Christian nor Moslem, with a few notable exceptions, invoked religion save as a cloak for secular political ends, but it was the ideological banner under which men fought and for which men can always be counted on to die' (p. 197).

Chapter Five

1. Most of the basic material about the translations from Arabic into Latin is to be found in Moritz Steinschneider's *Die europäischen Übersetzungen aus dem Arabischen bis Mitte des 17. Jahrhunderts*, originally published in the Proceedings of the Vienna Academy (1904, 1905) and reprinted at Graz in 1956. Complementing this is *Die hebräischen Übersetzungen des Mittelalters* (Berlin, 1893; Graz, 1956) by the same author. These deal with both scientific and philosophical writings. Much work has been done, however, subsequently, especially since the Second World War; and this greatly alters the picture at various points. It is now realized that the attribution of a version to a specific translator is often no more than later guesswork; and a thorough examination of all available manuscripts has thus become necessary. The results obtained so far are scattered through numerous articles, such as: 'Avicenna Latinus' by Marie-Thérèse d'Alverny in *Archives d'Histoire doctrinale et littéraire du Moyen Âge*, xxviii (1961), 281-316 with further references; J. F. Rivera, 'Nuevos datos sobre los traductores Gundisalvo y Juan Hispano', *Al-Andalus*, xxxi (1966), 267-80. What was known up to 1938 about the transmission of Arab science to Europe is summarized by Aldo Mieli in *La science arabe* (n. 3/1); and numerous later articles are listed in the additional bibliography to the reprint. *Arabic Thought and the Western World* by Eugene A. Myers (New York, 1964) is a strange compilation; after some unbalanced chapters on Arabic thought in general, there are lists of the translators and their translations into Latin, Hebrew, etc., but with inaccuracies and without any indication of the sources of the information or of the extent of the problems and uncertainties. The relevant section of Pearson's *Index Islamicus* is IV, c. iii.

A general account and evaluation of the influence of Arab science in Europe will be found in *Studies in the History of Mediaeval Science* by the historian Charles Homer Haskins (Cambridge, 1927). Cf. also George Sarton, *Introduction to the History of Science* (n. 3/1), vols. ii, iii. D. M. Dunlop's *Arabic Science in the West* (Karachi, n.d. ? 1958) is more recent and consists of four lectures originally given at Cambridge in 1953; special attention is given to Michael Scot, Albertus Magnus and Peter Abano and the School of Padua. For the European response to the new knowledge, an important study is that on *Robert Grosseteste and the Origins of Experimental Science* (Oxford, 1953) by A. C. Crombie. Georges Vajda, *Introduction à la pensée juive du moyen âge*, Paris 1947, gives an idea of the Jewish contribution.

2. The standard work on medieval universities and other schools is *The Universities of Europe in the Middle Ages* by Hastings Rashdall, new edition edited by F. M. Powicke and A. B. Emden, Oxford, 1936. For the work of Alfonso x cf. ii. 76-81, 90f. For the essential differences between the European university and the Islamic *madrasa* cf. George Makdisi, 'Muslim institutions of learning in eleventh century Baghdad', *Bulletin of the School of Oriental and African Studies*, xxiv (1961), 1-56; 'Madrasa and University in the Middle Ages', *Studia Islamica*, xxxii (1970), 255-64.
3. Cf. Hunke, *Allahs Sonne* (n. 1/1), 41-108. Reference may also be made to a translation of Pedro Alfonso's *Disciplina Clericalis* under the title *Die Kunst vernünftig zu leben* (Zurich, 1970); the translator, Eberhard Hermes, has added a long introduction on the man and his times.
4. Cf. *Legacy of Islam*, 344-54; Hunke, *Allahs Sonne*, 109-90. The work of Usāma ibn-Munqidh is translated by Philip K. Hitti as *An Arab-Syrian Gentleman and Warrior in the Period of the Crusades* (New York, 1929); see esp. pp. 162-7; the passage is reprinted in James Kritzeck, *Islamic Literature* (Harmondsworth, 1964), 217f. The fullest study is Heinrich Schipperges, *Die Assimilation der arabischen Medizin durch das lateinische Mittelalter*, (Sudhoffs Archiv, Beiheft 3), Wiesbaden, 1964.
5. The influence of the Islamic philosophers on medieval European thought is described in general histories of philosophy such as: Emile Bréhier, *Histoire de la philosophie*, vol. i, part 3 (Paris, 1931); Étienne Gilson, *La philosophie au Moyen Âge* (Paris, 1925) and *A History of Christian Philosophy in the Middle Ages* (London, 1955); F. J. Copleston, *A History of Philosophy*, vol. iii (London, 1953); Gordon Leff, *Medieval Thought from Saint Augustine to Ockham* (Harmondsworth, 1958); Philippe Wolff, *The Awakening of Europe* (The Pelican History of European Thought, 1) (Harmondsworth, 1968). The relevant sections of

De Lacy O'Leary's *Arabic Thought and its Place in History* (London, 1922) are now rather out-of-date. An important detailed study is that of Charles Homer Haskins, *The Renaissance of the XIIth Century* (Cambridge, Mass., 1933). Vincenzo M. Poggi in *Un classico della spiritualità musulmana* (Rome, 1967) devotes three chapters (pp. 53-133) to a study of the influence of al-Ghazālī's *Munqidh* on certain medieval writers.

Chapter Six

1. Most of what is said about the distorted image of Islam is based on Norman Daniel's careful study, *Islam and the West, the Making of an Image* (Edinburgh, 1960), where detailed references will be found. A brief survey of this material but in a wider context is given by R. W. Southern in *Western Views of Islam in the Middle Ages* (Cambridge, Mass., 1962).

   During the last thirty years much light has been thrown on the spread of the knowledge of Islam in Europe. Ugo Monneret de Villard collected much material in an extended essay, *Lo studio dell' Islam nel XII e nel XIII secolo* (Vatican, 1944). An important step forward was made by Marie-Thérèse d'Alverny in an article, 'Deux traductions latines du Coran au Moyen Age', *Archives d'histoire doctrinale et littéraire du Moyen Age*, xvi (1947-8), 69-131, following on her rediscovery of MS 1162 of the Bibliothèque de l'Arsenal, Paris. This twelfth-century manuscript contains the Toledan Collection and is indeed in all likelihood the original copy, made by the translators or for them. The collection is summarized by James Kritzeck in *Peter the Venerable and Islam* (Princeton, 1964), and the texts given of Peter's *Summary* and *Refutation*; there is also an account of Peter's life and of the translators. It is now generally accepted that the translator of the Qur'ān was Robert of Ketton (in Rutlandshire), also called Robert of Chester, but older books follow a mistake in the text and call him 'Retenensis'. The paper by Marie-Thérèse d'Alverny at the Spoleto Congress (Report, ii. 577-602), 'La connaissance de l'Islam en occident du IXe au milieu du XIIe siècle' is a survey of what was known to scholars up to 1964, and, like James Kritzeck's book, has further bibliographical information. Important also is her article in collaboration with Georges Vajda on 'Marc de Tolède, traducteur d'Ibn Tumart' (*Al-Andalus*, xvii [1952], 124-31), since Mark of Toledo had also translated the Qur'ān.

2. Among works about the growth of European self-awareness may be mentioned *Europe, the Emergence of an Idea* by Denys Hay (revised edition, Edinburgh, 1968). Arab influences on

Dante were noted by Miguel Asin Palacios in *La escatologia musulmana en la Divina Comedia* (Madrid, 1919; Eng. tr. 1926); the most authoritative study is Enrico Cerulli's *Il Libro della Scala e la questione delle fonti arabo-spagnole della Divina Commedia* (Vatican, 1949). The saying of Pico della Mirandola (p. 118) and that of the Spaniard at Salamanca are quoted from Dunlop, op.cit. (n. 5/1), 83,94.

3. Ibn Khaldūn, *The Muqaddimah*, tr. by Franz Rosenthal, 3 vols., London, 1958; see ii. 42-6, 101, 263. Muslim attitudes to the Crusades are described by G.E von Grunebaum in his paper entitled 'The World of Islam: the Face of the Antagonist' in *Twelfth-Century Europe and the Foundations of Modern Society*, edited by Clagett, Post and Reynolds (Madison, Wisconsin, 1961), 189-211, esp. 190f.
4. Southern, *Western Views* (n. 6/1), 79.

INDEX

The Arabic article al-, *with its variants*, an-, ash-, *etc.*, *is neglected in the alphabetical arrangement*

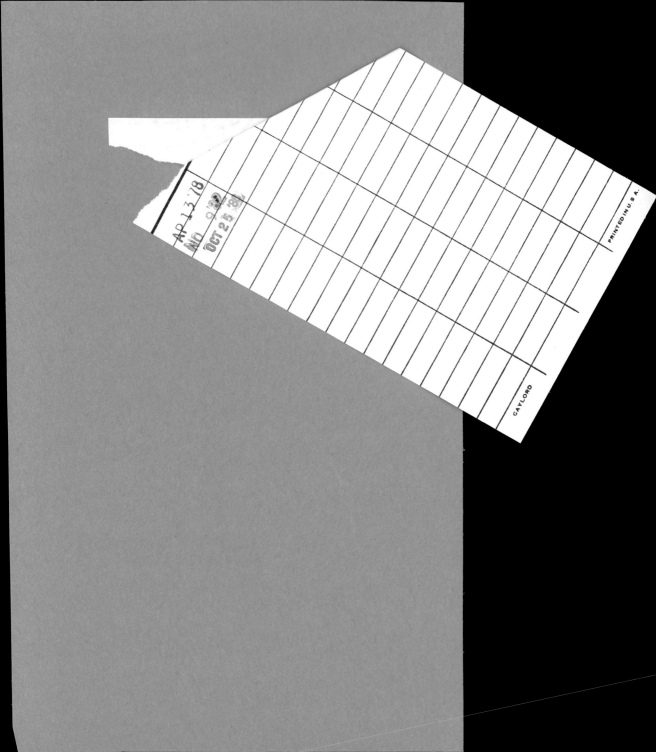